On Mo
Poetry

‌niversity Cent

On Modern Poetry

From theory to total criticism

Robert Rowland Smith

continuum

Continuum International Publishing Group

The Tower Building	80 Maiden Lane
11 York Road	Suite 704
London	New York
SE1 7NX	NY 10038

www.continuumbooks.com

British Library Cataloguing-in-Publication Data
A catalogue record for this book is available from the British Library.

ISBN: HB: 978-1-4411-6572-5
PB: 978-1-4411-7422-2

Library of Congress Cataloging-in-Publication Data
Smith, Robert Rowland.
On modern poetry : from theory to total criticism / Robert Rowland Smith.
p. cm.
Includes bibliographical references and index.
ISBN 978-1-4411-6572-5 (hardcover : alk. paper)– ISBN 978-1-4411-7422-2 (pbk. : alk. paper)– ISBN 978-1-4411-4976-3 (ebook pdf)– ISBN 978-1-4411-4852-0 (ebook epub)
1. Poetry, Modern–20th century–History and criticism–Theory, etc. 2. Modernism (Literature) I. Title.

PN1271.O5 2012
809.1'04–dc23

2011046644

Typeset by Fakenham Prepress Solutions, Fakenham, Norfolk NR21 8NN
Printed and bound in India

To Antonioni, il mellor fabbro

It must
Be the finding of a satisfaction, and may
Be of a man skating, a woman dancing, a woman
Combing. The poem of the act of the mind.

FROM WALLACE STEVENS, 'OF MODERN POETRY'

CONTENTS

ACKNOWLEDGEMENTS

For kind permission to quote from works to which they own the rights, I thank the following: Barque Press; Columbia University Press; Curtis Brown; David Higham Associates; Faber and Faber; Marion Boyars Publishers; New Directions; Oxford University Press on behalf of The British Province of the Society of Jesus; Penguin Books; University of Chicago Press; Yale University Press.

This book, though in its present form a distant relation of them, has its origin in lectures I gave in the 1990s during my Prize Fellowship at All Souls College, Oxford. Thanks to those who participated. More recently, I've had helpful feedback from Clare Birchall, and David Avital at Continuum has provided useful support. My inspiration has come from Tim Clark, Anthony Mellors, Jan Piggott, Jeremy Prynne, Denise Riley, Nick Royle and Ann Wordsworth; and among the dead from Paul de Man, Jacques Derrida, William Empson and Walter Pater. Chapeau!

INTRODUCTION

Below is a Seamus Heaney poem, published in 2010 by Faber and Faber:[1]

A Mite-Box

But still in your cupped palms to feel
The chunk and clink of an alms-collecting mite-box,
Full to its slotted lid with copper coins,

Pennies and halfpennies donated for
'The foreign missions' ... Made from a cardboard kit,
Wedge-roofed like a little oratory

And yours to tote as you made the rounds,
Indulged on every doorstep, each donation
Accounted for by a pinprick in a card –

A way for all to see a way to heaven,
The same as when a pinholed Camera
Obscura unblinds the sun eclipsed.

There is the poem. What is one supposed to do with it? Already we have a deal of information to sift, and not just in the verses themselves. For reasons that go beyond scholarly diligence, I have provided author, date and publisher: these too are avenues in.

Apart from anything else, the name 'Seamus Heaney' is a brand that says 'leading poet', 'professor', 'wise owl', 'institution', 'lyricist', 'Irishman', 'mainstream', 'successful', 'naturalist', 'human', 'warm', 'sensuous', 'avuncular', 'skilled', 'artisanal', 'earthy'. Had I left the name out, you, the reader, might have felt more tentative reading the poem, assuming you didn't already know who wrote it. But the name gave you, however fleetingly or subliminally, a promise of what to expect. In so doing, it will have either increased or decreased your alertness to the text – or both. Increased, because the work of a publicly endorsed poet is more likely to command your attention. Decreased, because the guarantee of quality invisibly engraved in such a name can blind one's critical faculties.

Either way, the connotations that come with the name 'Seamus Heaney' suggest that modern poetry might not be so 'modern' after all: they are far too reassuring. True, 'A Mite-Box' doesn't rhyme, the metre is irregular, its two sentences are not properly finished, and Heaney has dropped a neologism, 'unblinds', into the last line, but any modernity it can claim lies mainly in its date (2010). Published nearly a century after *The Waste Land*, it is no further down the track of poetic innovation. On the contrary, it lags some way behind T. S. Eliot's radical tableau of disjointed voices. In the vernacular, you might call it quite a 'traditional' poem. In my terms, it is a pre-modernist modern poem, implying that 'modern poetry' is a complex genre, if a genre at all.

Yet Heaney is published by Eliot's own publisher, Faber and Faber. Not just publisher: Eliot was closely involved with Faber the business as an employee, and later a director; Eliot's widow, Valerie, was to become a key shareholder. The names Eliot and Faber are as intertwined commercially as they are editorially. Thanks not least to Eliot money, derived from sales, and the Eliot name, Faber was able to establish itself as a leading poetry publisher in the UK and wider territories. When we talk about 'modern poetry', we are often signalling Faber poets, Heaney included. Considering Eliot's poetic legacy, the fact that Faber has tended subsequently to favour pre-modernist works – not just Heaney, but, say, Ted Hughes – is therefore a little ironic.

Not that Faber doesn't continue to publish Eliot himself or Ezra Pound, but on the whole Faber has become more conservative and, given its influence on the poetry market, so has that market. The conservatism isn't necessarily bad: it answers a demand for accessible poetry in schools, for example. Ted Hughes can be taught in a way that Ezra Pound cannot. Though verse by Hughes carries a share of literary allusion, it is nothing compared with the profusion of reference in Pound, a poet who is either saved for university or, as is increasingly the case, ignored. Better that schoolchildren be put on a pre-modernist modern diet than be put off altogether.

So 'modern poetry', the subject of this book, contains at least two strains of modern, as manifested in the two sides of Faber: one modernist like Eliot, the other pre-modernist like Heaney. Putting dates on it is arbitrary. Common practice will often use 'modern' to mean 1900 onwards, but I extend it back almost another hundred years to Keats, on the grounds that his poetry is about as far back as today's reader can go without starting to encounter diction that is challenging simply on account of its age. Even Keats, of course, can be difficult on these grounds. One tends to think of modernism as a decisive break with everything before it, but plenty of twentieth-century poetry continued to draw its inspiration from Tennyson or Hardy, say. My rule isn't hard and fast, but one consequence is that 'modernity' keeps moving forward, even as genres such as 'modernism' remain tagged to specific writers at specific dates.

Late modernism

I'll come back to the Heaney poem presently, but, having made a distinction between modernist and pre-modernist, am I obliged to say something about postmodernism? All 'ism's are odious but, as Kant said of metaphors, they do help us to think, even if they should be thrown away after use. I believe the lead to follow is that of Anthony Mellors, who prefers 'late modernism' to describe the hermetic style in poetry most vividly represented by J. H. Prynne.[2] Published by the shoestring independent, Barque Press, only a year prior to Heaney's 'A Mite-Box', here, for example, is Prynne's own take on a poem about a box:[3]

> Inside the tight closed box it was it was out
> a same summer box oh then at must closed on all
> or maybe often maybe open to one side glaze be
> in part to spill affirm parted along a rim ballast

That is the first stanza of what appears to be a six-stanza poem. I say 'appears to be' because each poem in the Prynne pamphlet entitled *Streak-Willing-Entourage-Artesian* has an identical format, lacks a title, and runs to the end of the page, so one isn't confident the 'collection' is not one long poem continued over 12 pages. The feeling of repetition, the sense of computer printout, is reinforced by a narrow font with the stippled look of binary code. As for what the poem means, and as for teaching what it means, there are hurdles to jump as high as anything thrown up by Eliot or Pound, and it is even more offensive to one's sense of literary decorum. If this is late modernism, it is the subculture to Faber's official poetry culture, continuing the Eliot/Pound agenda and upping the ante.

I used the word 'hermetic' above, and there is a strong sense in which late modernism, at least in Prynne form, is itself a 'tight closed box' which 'maybe open to one side' but maybe not. And so it is worth making another distinction, this time between two types of hermetic. *The Waste Land* is hermetic in the modernist sense of being replete with allusions that ask for investigation. When Eliot depicts a game of chess, we trace the reference back to Thomas Middleton. The mystery is solved, and the critic can proceed to considering how Eliot has adapted the Middleton text to his own ends.

What about the following Celan poem, as translated by Michael Hamburger?[4]

NO MORE SAND ART, no sand book, no masters.

Nothing won by dicing. How many
dumb ones?
Seventeen.

Your question – your answer.
Your song, what does it know?

Deepinsnow,
    Eepinnow,
        E – i – o.

This is hermeticism of a late modernist order that has little to do with decrypting literary reference – though it is certainly conceivable that the 'Nothing won by dicing', say, alludes to Mallarmé's 'Un Coup de Dés' ('A Throw of the Dice'), especially given the scattering of the words on the page.[5] But even if we could find sources for every word, we'd still founder on the enigma of the last three lines.

Marjorie Perloff dubs the poem 'hermetic and condensed',[6] and those three lines literally condense the language by wringing out the consonants. And yet 'condensed' implies it could be de-condensed, like you can rehydrate a dry sponge, and this is misleading. For a start, we already know what a rehydrated 'E – i – o' looks like, namely 'Deepinsnow'. So there is no mystery, and the phrase 'Deepinsnow', which condenses three words into one, is hardly hermetic – it's practically a cliché. At the same time, by deseeding the phrase of its consonants, 'E – i – o' does the inverse of what the Tetragrammaton does in removing the vowels from the name of the Lord, to make YHWH. As such, it suggests something either sacred or, because of the inversion, profane. This is not to be understood as a 'reference' to the Tetragrammaton but a display of language under analogous pressure to say the unsayable. In other words, 'E – i – o' averts to a structural limit that language runs up against as a mode of 'expression'. Hence perhaps 'NO MORE SAND ART, no book, no masters'. The ineffable is buried deep in snow. It's this second-order 'hermeticism' that among other things separates late modernism from hermetic modernist antecedents like Eliot and Pound.

Identity moderne

To modernist, pre-modernist and late modernist, I'll add a fourth genre, and then move on. What I call 'identity moderne' lies at the other, demotic end of the spectrum from late modernism. If 'expression' in late modernism bends back towards impossibility, identity moderne believes expression to be not just possible but mandatory. It is nothing if not a celebration of self-expression. There is even a route out of *The Waste Land* that sanctions it, for if Eliot's poem can be deemed an impersonal exhibit of fragments from the decline of the West, it can also be read as an introspective jeremiad, in which the pluriform phenomena embody a catatonic personal state. Identity moderne supports a democratic, individualist notion that everyone is unique, that everyone has a story, and that about these two propositions there is something inherently poetic.

The result is poems of a narrative, and especially confessional, style. Carol Ann Duffy would represent this category well. Here's the first half of her 'Valentine':[7]

Not a red rose or a satin heart.

I give you an onion.
It is a moon wrapped in brown paper.
It promises light
like the careful undressing of love.

Here.
It will blind you with tears
like a lover.
It will make your reflection
a wobbling photo of grief.

I am trying to be truthful.

We cannot assume an intrinsic connection between the narrative voice and the poet herself, but the poem does stage a scene between an I and a you. Duffy's ironic take on a valentine gift has a confessional air, and the line 'I am trying to be truthful' could serve as a motto for identity moderne: the desire to convey subjective feeling in an intense fashion that nevertheless keeps poetic artifice on a tight leash in case it compromises the sincerity. This is not to say a bit of wit and invention isn't admissible, as in the practical joke of substituting an onion for a red rose, and it's why I add the florid 'e' to the word 'modern', to make it 'identity moderne'. But such witticisms exist to adorn, not detract from, a sentiment that is unmockably subjective and sincere.

That is all fine except it runs the risk of becoming less poetic; of becoming a subspecies of narrative, identifiable as poetry only by its truncated lines, startling similes or well-spaced orchidaceous words. (Not that this is unwelcome by readers who tend to consider poetry not written in narrative or first-person terms as avant-garde or difficult – 'difficult' poetry was once the centrepiece of university literature courses, but has fallen behind narrative poetry and prose, as have the skills to unpack it.) Now, a poem patently can contain narrative elements, and the very origins of Western poetry in Homer suggest that the relationship between poetry and narrative is more than casual, so it's not a question of rounding up any poem with narrative elements and indicting it. And yet part of what makes poetry poetry is the right it can exercise not to assume narrative form. This does not mean it has to be cryptic, but one of the chief innovations attributable to modernist poetry was its hiving off of narrative. As you can relieve painting from its task of representing the world and still get a painting – abstract expressionism being the prime example – so you can take narrative away from poetry and it still stands. Arguably, like Celan's 'NO MORE SAND ART', it stands as more nakedly 'poetic'.

Lit crit vs Theory

I began by copying out Seamus Heaney's 'A Mite-Box', as if I were about to perform literary-critical surgery. Instead, I set off on questions of market and genre, and gestured towards the material conditions of the poem's production. That might suggest a Marxist or new historicist approach: were I an old-school critic, I would dive straight into the text, treating it as an aesthetic object in its own right. However, I am none of the above, and one of my aims with this book is to get beyond such factions. In the service of which, I defer a reading of Heaney's poem 'itself' again.

According to the stereotype, literary theory tends to turn up its nose at practical criticism, and vice versa. Hastily damning it as 'Leavisite', theory – or 'Theory' with a capital 'T' – considers that practical criticism or 'lit crit' treats poems in a historical vacuum, and suspects it of putting those poems on a pedestal like Keats' own Grecian urn. What's worse, practical criticism suffers the illusion, according to Theory, that the critical language it uses is transparent, disinterested and untouched by the machinations of ideology.

For its part, practical criticism sees Theory as a grandiloquent, self-regarding discourse that suppresses the specificity of the text in favour of general propositions consonant with the theory being brought to bear – as if it were less a matter of 'readings' than corroborations. It too detects in its rival a lack of appreciation for the historical context of the poem, especially when it comes to the biography of its author; and if, as in New Historicist approaches, history does get introduced, it still severs the link with the author, ascribing the poem's coming into being to a series of historical convergences that are, paradoxically, both necessary and contingent.

xviii   INTRODUCTION

What runs beneath this antagonism between Theory and practical criticism is a larger tension between cultures. Theory is 'continental' and more amenable to speculative or idealist thinking, with its peculiar amalgam, itself historically determined, of poetics, French post-structuralism, Marxist materialism, German idealism and psychoanalysis. Practical criticism hails from America and Britain where the empirical method is preferred, and where, nevertheless, a residual romanticism or, for want of a better phrase, pastoral idealism, prevails. Both are strange accidents of history. To put it crudely, if Theory likes poems and their readings to be more difficult than beautiful, practical criticism likes them to be more beautiful than difficult.

The implication is that, in all cases, the poetry suffers. Ideally, one would like to read accounts of poems that are not partisan, but free to move with the movement of the poem. After all, reading isn't reading if it doesn't allow itself to be surprised by a poem, by elements in it that a theory could not have anticipated, or which practical criticism doesn't brush aside as inconvenient to its attempt to aestheticize the text. This is not to claim that there will ever be a way of addressing poetry without its own blind spots, but it is to venture that more rounded – and more idiosyncratic – accounts of poetry might still be achieved.

In the meantime, this stand-off between Theory and practical criticism is as false as it is real, and like many enemies, they have more in common than either 'side' cares to admit. Take the notion of close reading, so prized by literary criticism, and turn to an essay by Paul de Man. Qua theorist, he is supposed to be away with the metaphysical fairies, and yet see how tenaciously precise, even pedantic is his reaction to these lines of Yeats:[8]

> ... we rode on,
> Where many a trumpet-twisted shell
> That in immortal silence sleeps
> Dreaming of her own melting hues,
> Her golds, her ambers, and her blues,
> Pierced with soft light the shallowing deeps.

De Man comments that:

> This image starts from the perception of an actual thing, the eye catching sight of the shells as the water grows shallow. The late

version (which dates from a 1933 edition) still strengthens this effect by means of the exact visual detail 'trumpet-twisted,' but it is clear from the unaltered line, 'Pierced with soft light the shallowing deeps', that the encounter with the natural, outward world has always been an essential part of the image. It grows, however, into much more than a descriptive or decorative detail. The transfer of the material attributes of shape and colour into consciousness, which makes up the perception, is accompanied by a symmetrical transfer of acts of consciousness into the object: the shell is said to be 'dreaming' and the verb 'pierced' changes the passive process of being perceived into an act of volition; by then, the shell has both imagination and will, the main faculties of a conscious mind, and it has received them from a mere figure of speech.

If this is Theory it is markedly rooted in the lexical matter of the text under consideration, right down to a scholarly exactitude over the editions being read. Far from avoiding the specifics of Yeats' text, de Man soaks in them. What is more, he deploys classic lit crit language such as 'The late version ... still strengthens this effect' where effect-strengthening is an aesthetic virtue to be noted and implicitly praised. In the world of literature, an 'effect' is pre-eminently aesthetic in that it causes us, the reader, to feel or to sense, which requires not just the literary skill of the author, but a refinement on our part.

Let's not be disingenuous, however. Before long de Man is reaching for terms like 'consciousness', 'volition' and 'material attributes', all lifted from a more philosophical than literary lexicon. When he asserts that 'the shell has both imagination and will, the main faculties of a conscious mind', readers of Kant and Schopenhauer will have their allusion glands instantly stimulated. De Man might well be nailing his argument firmly to the words on the page, but as he writes, a metaphysical atmosphere spreads over his essay as implacably as a bank of clouds, even if it is de Man's larger project to shoo all metaphysics away.

Which is the more important point: it's not that Theory embraces close reading, although it demonstrably does (point one), but that, contrary to the charges levelled against it, it eschews metaphysics (point two). Inspired by de Man and even more by Derrida, Theory begins with an aversion to all things metaphysical, on the grounds

that metaphysics so extols rationality (or 'logocentrism') that it is
blind to anything else. And poetry is a very good example of what
cannot be accounted for in exclusively rational terms. The oddity
in both de Man and Derrida is the rigour and intelligence they
bring to bear on texts they prove to defy their rigour and intelligence. To high theorist and literary critic alike, in fact, poetry
remains elusive. No matter how close they get to a poem through
aesthetic sensitivity or philosophical analysis, it never surrenders
all its secrets. The literary critic will ascribe this elusiveness on the
part of the poem to essential or transcendental mystery, the theorist
to an epistemological abyss at its heart, but both are content to be
servants, not masters, of literature.

Up to a point, anyway. Now consider this paragraph from F. R.
Leavis, nemesis of Theory, taken from his essay on Gerard Manley
Hopkins in *The Common Pursuit*:[9]

> Hopkins is the devotional poet of a dogmatic Christianity. For the
> literary critics there are consequent difficulties and delicacies. But
> there is something that can be seen, and said, at once: Hopkins's
> religious interests are bound up with the presence in his poetry of
> a vigour of mind that puts him in another poetic world from the
> other Victorians. It is a vitality of thought, a vigour of the thinking
> intelligence, that is at the same time a vitality of concreteness. The
> relation between this kind of poetic life and his religion manifests
> itself plainly in his addiction to Duns Scotus, whom, rather than
> St. Thomas, traditionally indicated for a Jesuit, he significantly
> embraced as his own philosopher. Of the philosophy of Duns
> Scotus it must suffice to say here that it lays a peculiar stress on
> the particular and actual, in its full concreteness and individuality,
> as the focus of the real, and that its presence is felt whenever
> Hopkins uses the word 'self' (or some derivative verb) in his
> characteristic way. 'Binsey Poplars' provides an instance where
> the significance for the literary critic is obvious. The poplars are

> All felled, felled, are all felled,

and Hopkins' lament runs:

> O if we but knew what we do
>   When we delve or hew –

Hack and rack the growing green!
  Since country is so tender
To touch, her being so slender,
That, like this sleek and seeing ball
But a prick will make no eye at all,
Where we, even where we mean
    To mend her, we end her
  When we hew or delve:
After-comers cannot guess the beauty been.

Leavis cites another five lines of 'Binsey Poplars' and leaves the paragraph
at that. It is as if Hopkins' verse so self-evidently proves Leavis' point
that spelling it out would be facile. Certainly there are moments of
detailed textual analysis elsewhere in the essay, but in this half a page
or so, we find lit crit – or at least the Leavisite version – at its most
expansive, its tone at its most masterful. The first sentence 'Hopkins
is the devotional poet of a dogmatic Christianity' is not entirely free
of dogma itself. Hopkins may well possess 'vigour of mind' but where
it is demonstrated in the extract from 'Binsey Poplars' is hard to put a
finger on. That word 'vigour' appears twice, along with 'vitality', as
though we are reading less about poetry, which in the scheme of things
is somewhat effeminate, than a non-specific moral exercise surging
with manly health. And Leavis seems to be claiming that the fact that
Hopkins uses the word 'self' in his poetry is evidence of an addiction to
Duns Scotus … We have left the ground of close reading and risen to
a suave and capacious dominance of the poetry being considered – the
very accusation laid against Theory by literary critics.

But perhaps close reading was never quite the aim. As Leavis
reveals in its preface, his book's title *The Common Pursuit* is
an abbreviation of a phrase of Eliot's – 'the common pursuit of
true judgment'. At first, Leavis emphasizes the word 'common',
suggesting that true judgement over literary material can best be
arrived at by collaborating with other readers, and he cites some
peers. But it doesn't ring true – the essays themselves feel too much
the work of a single hand – and a page later he ditches the word
'common', leaving us to infer that the key term is 'judgment'. And
by exercising judgement, it is the poet's character and sensibility
that are at stake, rather than the verse which gives them expression.

What is more, this Leavisite approach to poetry is more than a little
philosophical. Read again the sentence, 'It is a vitality of thought, a

vigour of the thinking intelligence, that is at the same time a vitality of concreteness.' Setting aside the Lawrentian masculinism, Leavis is saying how Hopkins' poetry forges two opposites, the abstract with the real, into one; a moment ago de Man was saying 'the shell has both imagination and will, the main faculties of a conscious mind', thus combining the concrete (shell) with the intellectual (imagination and will). Both men are describing the relationship between mind and matter, and poetry's unique genius for mediating between them. Poetry might well draw us into specific similes and images, but it is hard for gifted critics to resist the philosophical generalities that might be gleaned. To the mind of the critic of whatever school, poetry can easily turn into an intellectual object reflecting the critic's mind.

In short, the story of poetry criticism as rivalry between Theory and lit crit is a busted flush. Both are over-determined idioms that criss-cross each other, and the usefulness of a distinction between the two has expired. More useful would be to discuss individual critics than schools of criticism. Whatever, de Man wrote his last pieces in the early 1980s, and Leavis' words just quoted come from 1952. If there is a need for a new critical movement to inspire more than a single critic, I would call it that of total criticism. This would involve looking at a poem in the round, without pretending not to know about brand, font, market, and so on, as much as epistemology and aesthetics. It is a blessing or a curse of our own late modernity that we have such a wealth of information available, but we need to work with it. Bracketing off data as non-relevant looks increasingly untenable. That we'll ever include everything that could be said about a poem is no doubt an illusion, and a last-ditch attempt at winning back some of that mastery, but if they are to trade their secrets, poems need generous readers.

The almighty mite

In the light of that wider context of modernity and its critics, I come back to 'A Mite-Box':

> But still in your cupped palms to feel
> The chunk and clink of an alms-collecting mite-box,
> Full to its slotted lid with copper coins,

Pennies and halfpennies donated for
'The foreign missions' ... Made from a cardboard kit,
Wedge-roofed like a little oratory

And yours to tote as you made the rounds,
Indulged on every doorstep, each donation
Accounted for by a pinprick in a card –

A way for all to see a way to heaven,
The same as when a pinholed Camera
Obscura unblinds the sun eclipsed.

The poem concerns a mite-box for collecting alms. The box was
once associated with the 'you' in line 7 who is probably different
from the 'your' in line 1, which we assume is 'your' as in 'one's
own'. But it could be the same: it is slightly ambiguous. Ambiguous
too is whether the poem is an elegy. The past tense in 'as you made
the rounds' pricks in a way that might be different from plain
nostalgia, the mite-box conceivably become a relic not solely from
the charitable church but a formerly living entity; in which case
the idea in the first line of still being able to feel something, though
dead, would matter a lot. The uncertainty over who's who and what
has happened to prompt this meditation on a mite-box is thickened
by the poem's interrupted grammar and the three-quarters-saidness,
whereby words start mid-sentence ('But still in your cupped palms
...') or peter out ('donate for/The 'foreign missions' ...'). Yes, we
have 'a poem about a mite-box', but the incompletenesses serve to
shunt that poem a degree or two off its axis, causing a soft confusion
at the level of comprehension that we, the reader, are presumably to
take as reflecting that in the narrator's mind, as he or she gropes for
a 'way to see' some light in the dark, and shuffles through a mental
attic of piled-up memories and sentimental notions.

    In the hermeneutic gloom, it is the mite-box itself that is the
thing to hold on to and marvel at. Because it is a relic apparently
rediscovered after long neglect, it gives off a musty, antiquarian
feel which, despite the box's being home-made, lends a rare value.
Indeed, this notion of significant worth wrought from a throwaway
object, something large got from something little, is the poem's
principal trope. Behind it lies the story of the 'widow's mite', as
told in the Gospel of Mark, King James Bible:[10]

And Jesus sat over against the treasury, and beheld how the people cast money into the treasury: and many that were rich cast in much.

And there came a certain poor widow, and she threw in two mites, which make a farthing.

And he called unto him his disciples, and saith unto them, Verily I say unto you, That this poor widow hath cast more in, than all they which have cast into the treasury:

For all they did cast in of their abundance; but she of her want did cast in all that she had, even all her living.

The lesson is how a small contribution counts for a great deal, laid out in a story behind which in turn stands a powerful Christian doctrine – perhaps *the* Christian doctrine – of multiplication: bountiful spiritual dividends leveraged from modest acts of earthly virtue; a few loaves of bread cloned to feed the 5,000; the meek inheriting the earth; the word of God spread via 'foreign missions' from 12 disciples to multitudes around the Mediterranean and beyond. It is multiplication per se which is the miracle – the mite grown mighty – and Christianity's defining promise. By moving from minor to major, Heaney's poem pursues a correspondingly miraculous (il)logic, the coppers potentially becoming great rewards, pennies from heaven, at a price-point that is indeed 'a way for all to see a way to heaven', and so get a return on their spiritual speculation.

The logic of multiples inheres in the very concept of the poem: Why write about a mite-box unless it has import larger than its diminutive dimensions? And now the concept gets turned into language. The figure of littleness is set with the title, the 'mite' of the mite-box being that small coin donated for a worthy cause; and continued with the pennies, halfpennies and coppers that are the smallest units of currency. Then a 'cardboard kit' evokes a reproduction in miniature. After which we have the oratory so 'little'. The 'pinprick' by which the pennies are added up – many a mickle makes a muckle – is a tiny mark that is half-repeated by the camera's pinhole, and it is here that we explicitly get the uplift from small to great, the pinhole opening into vistas unforeseen. In this hand-sized thing, a mere mite-box, says Heaney, we can spy something grand and see our way to heaven. We can peer out from the chunk and clink of this earthly prison, through the slot to the sun, now unblinded, eclipsed but more intense as a result. It is heaven in a mite of sand, a minor magnificat.

There is a meta discourse too, to do with the poem qua poem. In Chapter 3 below, on objects, I make the point at greater length, but an object in poetry is rarely just an object. Often it stands as a metaphor of the poem itself (as in the 'tight closed box' of late modernism), something free-standing and framed that merits attention in its own right. A box is especially significant in that a poem makes a square or oblong on the page that opens into a third dimension through its suggestion of semantic depth. In Heaney's poem, the box is filled with coins which, to use a phrase from de Man, function as 'allegories of reading', i.e. we read the poem and in so doing put in our two cents' worth, our contribution to get it whirring with meaning. In a parallel to that spiritual yield of everything from nothing, producing meaning is magical: it is conjuring thoughts from mute glyphs on the page, a miracle of multiplication at the level of sense. Though poems may be small, mere mites, they are saturated, like religious fetishes, with our hopes for their significance. As readers, we make a votive offering: we put money into the slot and wait for something meaningful to happen.

This silly superstitiousness reminds us that meaningful doesn't always equate to rational. In the mind-bending logic of 'unblinds the sun eclipsed', Heaney engages with what slips off the edge of reason. If in Christianity the way to heaven turns logic on its head – a camel getting through the eye of a needle more easily than the rich man, a pinhole too straitened for anything to squeeze through – in this last line Heaney shows how poetry too veers away from reason, and so suggests an affinity between the magic of religion and the magic of poetry. For there is a point at which all the pinpricks on the card add up to more than the sum of their parts and, as in a pinhole camera, the maths flips over. Now we are in an upside-down world, the logic gone topsy-turvy with the – What are they? Single, double or even triple? – negatives in 'unblinds the sun eclipsed'. This is why Heaney's account of accounting is a not entirely reliable account, and we, the reader, must suffer those ambiguities. It is a poem, not a recounting. The difference between poetry and prose gets demonstrated in poetry's camera-obscura genius not just for focusing on the tiny and projecting it on a larger screen, but turning it upside down. Where a prose narrative keeps going with the pinpricks – and then this, and then that – accounting for every line in the budget, the poem takes us inside its own endarkened shoebox cinema and shows us a little scene, some magic theatre, of luminous non-sense. And so this 'pre-modernist poem' borrows a little from modernism's letting-go of narrative.

There are further reasons why the box is magic, and defies the laws of gravity. It gets touted round every doorstep but resembles the oratory from which it has come. For the donor, it is like slotting money directly into the body of the church, thus shortening the distance between representer and represented, which ought, according to the classical rules of mimesis, to be kept a cognitive distance apart. In effect, Heaney presents us with literary transubstantiation whereby the metaphor is more than metaphorical, and rather uncannily real. Just as in the Catholic dogma under which Seamus was raised, where Communion wine is the actual blood of Christ, so the mite-box doesn't merely represent the oratory: by being a scale-version of it, it transmutes into the real thing, the 'cupped palms' a chalice. The reality is reinforced by the 'But still ...' at the poem's start, an interjection that is a rhetorical reminder of what is real. 'But still ... to feel': sensuous reality in the midst of representation and allegory. And if the poem is the box just as the box is the oratory, then the poem itself, flimsier than a pack of cards with a wedge-shaped roof, might just take on substance.

The meta-meta discourse concerns the poem qua poem in relation to other poems. A box with a hole makes not just a camera but a lyre, and 'A Mite-Box' thrums with earlier poets. That phrase 'But still ... to feel' has something of Hopkins – not 'Binsey Poplars', but the Terrible Sonnets. There is Yeats perhaps in the phrase 'a way to heaven', and in the quality of wonder, in the cadence that buoys it along, I feel the tone and rhythm of Yeats' 'Lapis Lazuli'. In 'unblinds the sun eclipsed' there is a wink at John Donne, in the 'cupped palms' you overhear Juliet flirting with Romeo, in 'chunks and clinks' an unslayable Beowulf, and in the 'as when' we even get Virgil. Part of what makes a poem a poem is that its frame is as leaky as it's firm: it is porous to other poets. Broadly I hold with Eliot's nostrum that mature poets steal rather than imitate, because there is always a risk in poetry that it merely channels its influences. But *being* influenced is conceivably a part of its nature. A poem forms an echo chamber, a vibrating requoting, more or less conscious, of earlier poems which themselves were twittering with bit-quotes. It tunes into the literary polyphony and selects a segment of voices. Not to mention how 'mature' poets effectively quote themselves and thus achieve a 'voice'. Hence the signature Heaney material: compound words ('alms-collecting mite-box', 'Wedge-roofed', as well as 'pinprick' and 'pinholed'), passive verbs/adjectives ('cupped', 'slotted', 'donated', 'made', 'indulged', 'accounted', 'eclipsed') and a reliance on Anglo-Saxon diction in all its flat-earth wariness of Latinism – 'pennies and halfpennies', especially. The '-ed' endings (as well as 'lid') keep knocking out a woodiness that is named more directly in 'cardboard' and 'card'. Heaney is also reprising Heaney.

Were I to conjecture what this poem was working through – beneath its surface content – I'd say it was the idea of the hand. Yes, the hand that holds. The idea starts with 'still in your cupped palms'. We then have 'collecting' in line 2. The reference to pennies necessarily involves the hands as what counts them up, just as the words 'donation' and 'donated' are more or less unthinkable, as terms for giving, without assuming the play of hands that give. The 'cardboard kit' needs hands to assemble it, and 'to tote' the hands to carry. The 'foreign missions' are about lending a hand. 'Wedge-roofed' imitates the praying hands – here's a church, here's a steeple – that previously were cupped. The camera is a handheld device, and unblinding the sun suggests the hand shading the eyes. (Even the previous poem in the collection begins with 'Seeing the bags of meal passed hand to hand'.) Mainly these are hands as the agency of giving and receiving – that's one meaning for the phrase 'human chain' which is the book's title – and thus the conduit between every doorstep, between people in a community. They are also the mechanism operated by people to signal a relationship between themselves and God in a church – the 'cupped palms' again.

But because of the richness of allusion both to religious and secular tropology, one wonders if this hand is also the poet's hand, Heaney working through the tradition of poetry and making it his own, a master poet who retains the workmanlike humility of an apprentice – in order to become what Eliot, his predecessor Faber poet, called 'il miglior fabbro': the better faber, the better poet, the better smith.

A word on 'total criticism'

Having somewhat coyly referred to 'total criticism', I'd like to end this beginning with some more explicit remarks. We're at a point where more poetry is being written than published, let alone read, mainly because poetry has come to be considered so much as an outlet for personal feelings – the poem as the stylized mode of the journal entry. Even among poetry that does get published – and there is a parallel with recent art – the emphasis on the recording of subjective experience is overwhelming. This emphasis lowers the technical requirements for writing a poem. You don't have to be able to master form if the content is sufficiently moving. These reduced demands on poet translate into a reduced demand on reader. Poetry that doesn't yield immediate gratification in terms of a life story, a conflicted identity, a subjective experience full of pathos or drama, gets pushed into the 'too difficult' pile.

At the same time, we have poets like Heaney whose poetry has a genuine depth demanding close attention, even if it often gets consumed as just the sort of confessional fare I am deploring. We also have poets like Prynne, who never gets mistaken for anything other than very serious indeed, and who is not at all popular. So there is an undeniable need for some kind of considered response to recent poetry; and of course the poetry of yesteryear, that of the canon, is hardly finished with yet.

But the criticism of poetry finds itself in an odd place, expected either to approach all poetry as a species of personal narrative – which leaves that criticism little room other than to comment on the personality behind it, and overlooks what is poetic about poetry – or to cling to the technical literary-critical competences that, thanks not least to I. A. Richards, defined it in the early twentieth century and that were extended so vigorously by Paul de Man. Just as the opposition between lit crit and Theory now needs to be laid aside, this choice between soft indulgence and hard analysis must be overcome.

What I propose instead, and what distinguishes what I am provisionally calling a 'total criticism', is a balance of analytic irony and imaginative empathy. By 'analytic irony' I mean that the criticism of poetry should endeavour to be as precise, careful and rigorous as anything in Richards, Empson or de Man. It must avail itself of the tools of prosody, rhetoric, linguistics and etymology that are essential for any claim to tradecraft. That is the 'analytic' part of 'analytic irony'. The 'irony' kicks in with the recognition that notwithstanding the advances made by those distinguished critics – and acknowledging that of the three de Man was especially aware of the fact – the criticism of poetry can never be a pure science. My reasons for stating this include the standard one that 'pure science' is an illusion even in science, if what is meant by 'pure science' is an objectivity cleansed of the interests of the observing subject. On the grounds that poetry is a highly affective art form, like other art forms it takes this distortion in the relationship between itself and its reader further – into the realm of transference, more or less in the Freudian sense. The analysis of poetry, like the analysis of an analysand on the couch, can't help but enter into a relay of projections: the difference being that the projections go mainly from reader to poem. But they also go the other way, in the sense that a given poem can appear to be communicating different things on different readings and with different emphases, and so producing different responses in the reader. That said, if the notion of 'reader response' implies something very cognitive or phenomenological or hermeneutic, I should correct it. The irony in analytic irony – and this is where it begins to merge with 'imaginative empathy' – is the recognition that poetry generates reactions at other levels, especially the emotional and affective, and even the somatic. It engages the reader's faculties in a way that both sweeps them together – activating the relationship between thought and feeling with new intensity – and displaces them. By 'irony' I mean the way in which the thoughtful analysis of a poem gets distracted by the feelings that poem produces, even as it tries to integrate them, successfully or otherwise, within the analysis.

As for 'imaginative empathy', this is the stance towards a poem that, rather than bearing down from above or looking from a safe distance, comes alongside it. If we can't account for a poem entirely in scientific terms, and if merely appreciating it for what it says about its author is too 'soft', then we should be aiming instead to support the poem in reaching the effect it has aimed for. I would liken imaginative empathy to the attitude involved in completing an unfinished symphony or novel, with the cardinal proviso that this is still criticism, not creation. Nicolas Abraham wrote an 'imaginatively empathetic' sixth act to *Hamlet*, which was nonetheless still in the mode of criticism: I think it is a valid model.[11] Criticism should still be criticism, even if its distance from a poem is irredeemably compromised. Imaginative empathy – which I have tried to demonstrate as far as I can in the second part of this book – involves occupying a middle ground between analytic distance and non-critical endorsement. In particular, it means falling in with the pace, mood or style of a given poem and elaborating it in discursive, associative terms. Some will scorn it for riffing too much on the poem in question, but for me the criticism always remains the servant of the poem, and not the other way round, whatever gratification the riffing affords for writer or reader.

So why 'total'? These sound like highly qualified approaches to the criticism of poetry, and besides, the word 'total' comes uncomfortably close to 'totalizing' and 'totalitarianism' (let alone 'total football') none of which is likely to earn much approval. But imaginative empathy can work only if it opens itself as much as possible to everything about the poem that might be pertinent. Theory became extraordinarily squeamish about being 'psycho-biographical', but in my view the fact of the author, not only in terms of biography and presumed intent, but even down to the writing body, must always be taken into account – even if the poetic involves a resistance to narrative and history. Let's use all the means available to us, not because poems need to be squashed with the data we readers and critics might bring forward, but because we are better equipped to resonate with a poem in all its unique strangeness if we have lined up every resource we can in that service. This doesn't mean that every reading needs to rehearse every conceivable fact and thought about a text, but it does mean excluding nothing in principle.

A last word about value judgements: We need to find a way of reintroducing value judgements into the study of literature, despite the obvious objection that all judgements are subjective, driven by motives often as unconscious as conscious, and serving the interests of the judge. For me, the point about judgement is that it is *judgement*, i.e. not a matter of asserting a truth (as in the common pursuit of '*true*' judgement), or even of claiming authority, but of exercising discretion and discernment, based on the particular critic's skill, scholarship and experience.

PART ONE

Themes

1

Two or three lines through modern poetic theory

I would like to offer two or three different genealogies for modern poetic theory. If they conflict, so much the better, because although it is always possible and occasionally helpful to create strong, single narratives – such as my own account in the Introduction of pre-modernist modern, etc. – we have to remember there will always be counter-examples. My 'lines through' modern poetic theory is therefore to be understood in two ways, as both 'paths through' and 'crossings out'.

Some caveats

But before embarking on these genealogies, there is an obstacle to confront in the form of a contradiction between poetry and the very idea of a genealogy. Genealogy implies history and the linking over time between entities that enjoy a family resemblance. Poetry, by contrast – or rather, the poem – harbours a resistance to time, and so to both history and the genealogies by which history is sometimes articulated.

In what sense does the poem harbour a resistance to time? In the Introduction, I talked about a defining privilege enjoyed by the poem, namely its right not to include narrative elements. For sure, poems can be narrative in style, but in so far as a poem that lacks narrative features remains a poem, narrative does not belong to its core. A poem can dispense with narrative and still be 'poetic' – which implies that the narrative elements of a narrative poem are not those elements that make it poetic either. What is poetic about a poem includes its right to eschew narrative, even as it tells stories. And in its right to eschew narrative, poetry stands back from the temporality, or at least the illusion of temporality, on which narrative depends. Narratives (stories) work by stringing events together in sequence (even if the sequence is toyed with), thus creating a sense of time passing, so if poetry has no intrinsic connection with narrative, it probably has no intrinsic connection with temporality defined as the passage of time. It might instead be defined by a-temporality, by posting itself beyond time's outer edge.

To illustrate my point, I turn to Charles Tomlinson's 'Maine Winter':[1]

Ravenous the flock
who with an artist's
tact, dispose
their crow-blue-black
over the spread of snow –

Trackless, save where
by stalled degrees
a fox flaringly goes
with more of the hunter's caution than
of the hunter's ease.

The flock
have sighted him, are his match
and more, with their artist's eye
and a score of beaks against
a fox, paws clogged, and a single pair of jaws.

And they mass to the red-on-white
conclusion, sweep

down between
a foreground all snow-scene and a distance
all cliff-tearing seascape.

Tomlinson offers us a clear narrative of crows killing a fox. So clearly is the narrative a narrative that it will even use the word 'conclusion' in the last stanza. But the narrative isn't everything, and if it was, the poem could have been abbreviated to a few unadorned words such as 'Twenty crows identify a single fox in the snow and kill it for food'. Now, all sorts of non-narrative elements come together in this poem, the most fundamental unstated in the lines themselves, namely the play on the collective noun for crows being a 'murder'. The poem concerns a murder by a murder of crows, and this 'pun', if that is the right term, serves as the poem's operating conceit, supported by another, in-poem pun on 'ravenous' ravens, who belong to the crow family (it's an 'unkindness' of ravens). Being a conceit, an intellectual construct, a picture of an idea, it wears no narrative clothes. And there are other non-narrative elements strewn throughout. But my point about poetry's constitutional ability to turn away from narrative and into the atemporality of the image is best caught in those very words 'And they mass to the red-on-white/ conclusion', because the conclusion to the story is held momentarily in suspense by 'red-on-white'. It is a suspense that the poem could have sustained indefinitely without damaging its status as a poem; it could even have enhanced it. No doubt the phrase 'red-on-white' lends the narrative dramatic intensity, but paradoxically what makes the phrase intense is that it stuns the narrative as a predator stuns its prey. As the crows kill the fox, 'red-on-white' momentarily kills the narrative, making a statement and an image of bloody death that separates itself from and hovers above the narrative that continues beneath it. In this sense, the fox's blood seeping so artistically, as Tomlinson insists, into the snow, becomes a print of the poem as poem. The snow absorbs the fox's blood and stands as an emblem of this poem, and perhaps all poems – a permanent stain, especially a stain that is artistically coloured by the artist crows. This artistic bloodstain speaks to the death of the narrative within the life of the poem, an image that fixes itself not just in the snow but in the reader's mind of which the snow stands as a working correlative. The snow freezes time, and in it the artistic or poetic red-on-white makes its murderous mark.[2] That is what remains beyond the conclusion: the image survives the narrative. In contrast to the novel, in which the narrative generally survives or simply dominates the image, poetry launches these image-balloons that take the poem with it, so to speak, up and away from its narrative field. Hence the poem's detachment from time.

To be clear, it takes time to write a poem, as it does to read it; the poem's words proceed in an order from beginning to end, such that every poem, like every other text, has a basic, lexical 'temporality' to it. But because it can without jeopardy reject narrative time, the poem harps towards fixity, and most typically towards the fixity of the image – as if the poem were more photograph than movie. In Chapter 4, on voice, I shall explore the implications of this link between the poem and the image, and the poem's photographic desire to become light: for now what matters is the poem's atemporal stillness.

How can we relate a history of poetry when the poem at the heart of the poem, which stands outside of time, doesn't count as a historical object? Of course, poems can be and are classified according to author, just as they can be and are classified according to genre or date, and so on, but what is being classified in such classifications is not the poem so much as its contextual features. The fact that histories of poetry exist suggests that what they record are cultural artefacts and values rather than a history of the poem, which it might not be possible to relate at all. Because the poem doesn't belong to history, it doesn't belong to other poems in a genealogy. Indeed poems cannot really belong to each other, even where written by the same hand. The poem that sits at the heart of all poems, be they narrative or otherwise, is detached from history, time and genealogy. I am not saying the poem 'transcends' these considerations, because the gift of detachment is not necessarily superior – it is rather a turning away. Yes, poems can populate themselves with images taken from history, just as they can project representations of real life, but their privilege is to do without such pageantry. Or, to be more precise, when a poem incorporates narrative elements, when it portrays real or imaginary events taking place in time, such elements and events are not to be understood as having been *represented* by the poem. The poem does not reflect anything exterior to it, anything that exists in real or imaginary time. Its originary detachment means that the contents of a poem, however narrative, temporal or phenomenal they might appear, begin on the poem's inside, not its outside. The poem's object, if you will, is always itself. It is self-involved. Every poem is that poem's autobiography.

It's a notion that must come under especially intense attack from the genre of elegy, for what concerns itself more with the outer world than the elegy that commemorates the life of a living soul? How can a poem be 'autobiographical' when it treats of the biography of another? Think, for example, of Auden's elegy for Freud, which opens with the lines:[3]

> When there are so many we shall have to mourn,
> when grief has been made so public, and exposed
>   to the critique of a whole epoch
>   the frailty of our conscience and anguish,
>
> of whom shall we speak? For every day they die
> among us, those who were doing us some good,
>   who knew it was never enough but
>   hoped to improve a little by living.
>
> Such was this doctor.

With that last phrase, Auden names a deceased human being, 'this doctor', Dr Freud. Ostensibly, Auden has written a poetic biography, an elegiac obituary, of the founder of psychoanalysis. The poem could not exist without the existence of its subject, the Viennese doctor, and to this extent the poem depends on the phenomenal world, the world of reality and of real beings. And yet this poem concerns itself not with the biologic entity that is or was Freud, but an image of it. So what? An image has the opportunity to be an image only in so far as it can do without that of which it is the image. If an image remained tied to its corresponding being in the real world, the poem would die with the death of that being. The poem would die with the death of Freud. But this is not the case. The image of Freud doesn't require a living or even a real Freud to underwrite it, leaving the poem to occupy itself with that image on its own terms. The image is a poetic possibility that detaches itself from the temporal lives of human beings.

Auden's poem then thematizes this logic by drawing attention to the randomness according to which we commemorate this dead person rather than another: choosing Freud to remember is arbitrary given the countless number of the dead, and because of the sheer number, there's no certainty that it is Freud himself who gets recollected. Out of the 'so many we shall have to mourn', his image presses itself upon the memory of the poet, but the very multitude from which he stands out undermines the clarity of his eminence. The attempt to bring Freud into special relief gets superseded by the elegiac desire to commemorate for its own sake, to write an elegy: the subject of the genre cannot compete with the genre itself. The vision with which the poem views its subject is at best peripheral, for the subject serves mainly as the occasion for the verse which then busies itself with its own creation. It turns away from the time of human beings and towards the image of what it supposedly celebrates.

Not bestowed with external data, poetry has to work to give itself its own object, and an appropriative tension results. In this experience of concentration, the poem has also to hold off from itself what is not its own. The poem tries to neutralize or purify the space around it, and strives to be a category of one. Again, mistaking this tension for a transcendental quality is tempting, hence the sloganeering about the 'timelessness' of poetry (the contempt for such slogans helped to organize some Marxist literary criticism as well as its spin-off, the New Historicism). When I talk about the quasi-uniqueness of the poem I too am keen to keep away from asserting a transcendental status for it, a 'timeless quality'. What I would say instead is that the poem occupies itself with something specific to it, its own 'moment', if you like, but that since this moment is not empirical in the sense of being a datum, it is hard to set it within an ordinarily historical schema. One of the reasons why there is so much anxiety about 'historicizing' poetry, and literature in general, is no doubt the possibility that there is nothing essentially historical about either; that their conditions, conditions of production, are conditional in only a limited sense.

And yet there is another side to the story. For all this irreducible detachment, and despite its founding right to turn away, as an artefact the poem does achieve that cultural value I mentioned. While, on the one hand, the poem is properly 'aesthetic' in the sense of winning exemption from historicist assimilation of it; on the other hand, the autobiographical act whereby it establishes itself as a poem is one which leaves a trace, in that the poem posits itself as a text in time. It is this positing – equally irreducible – that prevents the poem from assuming the transcendental identity to which its aesthetic nature, on its own, would lead. After all, a purely transcendental entity, like a Platonic form, would not be legible in the world, except through a device such as anamnesis – the not-forgetting of the ideal – which hardly provides secure knowledge. The pure poem could only ever come to us in dreams or unreliable transcendental memories. To become legible, to become anything at all, the poem's autobiographical involution has to be balanced with, as it were, a biographical openness. The poem takes on a life that can be documented in time, and thus re-enters the domain of genealogy.

Does this suggest that in this domain, we might never capture the 'poem in itself'? Well, the turning-away of the poem doesn't leave a residue in the form of any content – the content is all in what is posited, in the text. So no. The poem's autobiographical resistance to history should not be understood in the sense of a secret to be unlocked. It is merely its right to be poetic, to deploy language in a way that can do without narrative, that can embrace the image, its own images, with impunity. The poem is pre-assigned to the image, committed to it, and it is the commitment that counts. At the same time, it can and has to coexist with the text that it posits, the text that exists in time as cultural artefact. And without wishing to oversell it, this is why what I am calling total criticism might be a more adequate way of dealing with poetry. In that it calls for both an aesthetic or quasi-transcendental along with a contingent, pragmatic or historical approach to poems, it reflects every poem's two conceptual parents – being in the world and not being in the world.

The tradition

With these caveats in mind, I take Eliot and Pound as authors of a first genealogical 'line' through modern poetic theory, even though doing so is to bypass Mallarmé, who is arguably more modern, more revolutionary and more pivotal than either. But I choose Pound and Eliot because they themselves were so consumed with genealogical questions, especially in the guise of 'the tradition'.

In his essay of 1913 on the subject, Pound writes that 'the tradition is a beauty which we preserve and not a set of fetters to bind us'.[4] It is a phrase I want to dwell on. In the face of the threat of binding us that is posed by the tradition, Pound is venturing an alternative interpretation, namely that the tradition is 'a beauty'. Enjoyment is what the tradition promises, not enslavement. Why would Pound feel the need to push back in this way? Presumably because the weight of poetic tradition, by 1913, has come to appear stifling, and Pound is sensitive to his late arrival in that tradition. It probably stifles for two reasons. First because the Victorian and Edwardian poetry that furnishes the nearest backdrop to his own craft has lost its energy. With the exception of the French symbolists, nineteenth-century poetry has degenerated into what is at best post-Romantic sentiment or neo-gothic fantasy and at worst drawing-room whimsy. Secondly because Pound's erudition, his super-awareness of classical and medieval poetry in particular sets off a din in his head that risks 'fettering' his own creative process. If the tradition threatens to bind us, it is because one is so acutely aware of it, and the threat is only sharpened by Pound's ambition to innovate.

Against this threat, Pound opposes the notion of tradition as a beauty to be preserved. The metaphor evokes an embalming, a chemical fixing of the beautiful, with Pound either as taxidermist or Renaissance courtier fussing to preserve the beauty of an aged lady. Out of what did such a fantasy arise? Pound's need to preserve was perhaps mobilized by his horror of increase and excess. There were, for instance, his crazy attempts to persuade Mussolini into circulating a new coinage in Fascist Italy, made of vegetable matter.[5] The idea was that the currency's value would expire with its own highly perishable lifespan, meaning that money could no longer be made out of money, thus preserving an original and ideal value. By the same token, Pound would rail against the ethos and practice of usury. So that when he speaks of preserving a tradition in poetry, he appears to be speaking about preserving an ideal value like money that doesn't accrue the supplementary, specious value we call interest. Preservation is the preserving of a death – hence the embalming – the death which is all the more emphatic in something that does not grow. Like the poetic tradition, money should remain fettered, ironically, to its original value. And if preserving the tradition is ironic in that it represents a fetter of its own, it also represents an excess. The tradition has to be preserved, but since the preserving of the tradition must by definition follow after that tradition, the act of preserving itself generates superfluity.

Nevertheless, the tradition has to be preserved, like money, leaving no surplus, and the stipulation carries through to Pound's notions of what a poem should be – a construct without excrescence. It explains why Pound was to become so enamoured of imagism, which is nothing if not the doctrinaire attempt to make word match thing exactly. Like the perishable coin, the word equals absolutely and unvaryingly the value of the thing it describes; the exchange rate is fixed. Here is the famous and perhaps necessarily brief poem called 'In a Station of the Metro', perfectly demonstrating that doctrine:[6]

IN A STATION OF THE METRO

The apparition of these faces in the crowd;
Petals on a wet, black bough.

One sentence, two lines, no verbs, one image in 'reality' (faces) and another to which those faces are likened (petals). The economy is striking. Imagism tries to close the intolerable speculative gap that can always be opened where the relation of value to thing falls apart. Just as the tradition is to be preserved from supervening elements, so the poem that makes up the tradition is best if stripped down to essentials.

On my account of the poem as independent in principle of narrative, Poundian imagism might seem to provide the most poetic of poems. The exclusion of any verb in 'In a Station of the Metro' forestalls narrative progression, even if the image suggests a degree of movement as the faces jostle in the middle distance, and even if there's a transience suggested by petals on a bough. However, I am not arguing that a poem ought not to include narrative: I am merely saying that its entitlement not to is constitutive. Besides, the tension between image and narrative in a poem – as in the Tomlinson above – scarcely undermines that poem, not least because of the dramatic fillip it gives. Rather, that tension allows the image to stand out, like the face on a pound coin. Part of what makes 'In a Station of the Metro' so penetrating is that the image achieves its effect of bas-relief because the narrative still finds its way into the poem through those proxy forms, those quasi-narratives – the sense of faces moving and the Japanese-cherry-blossom romanticism of falling petals. The fact that the poem is set in a station of the metro also furnishes a background movement – urban transit that blurs along the commuter tracks as faces float like ghosts in front of them. If the poem preserves, and if the poet preserves the tradition, they achieve their value by rescuing the image from the narrative that would otherwise detain it.

The Poundian stress on economy in poetry itself continues a tradition, associated with the Renaissance, which endorses 'measure' because 'measure is treasure'. A poem is obliged to be condensed, whereas narrative, or at least prose, should be transparent. But these terms are not so straightforward. You could say that Poundian imagism isn't condensed at all, because being condensed implies that the equation between word and thing has got out of whack, with too few words for the thing being imaged. And yet – or is it the same thing? – there is a richness to 'In a Station of the Metro' which swells towards excess rather than economy; besides, measure is treasure because studded with precious metals, i.e. words and phrases that hold more value than their weight on the page, so to speak. Pound's poem isn't just functional, it is beautiful. Hence the other aspect of his edict: the tradition is not just to be preserved, but is a *beauty* to be preserved. Preserving beauty means preserving something already greater than the sum of its parts, already possessing an excess value – which renders the preserving of it a somewhat futile task. The archivists of the poetic tradition have both to keep poetry as it is and allow its excessive appeal, its beauty, to manifest. Like money, the beautiful poem attracts interest; it was already on the way to surpassing its first valuation.

So it is as if to manage its bountiful loveliness that Pound says that 'the tradition is a beauty which we preserve', which is also a call for chastity and a longing for return; and return he does, compulsively, through different poetic genealogies – epic, Provençal, Chinese, Victorian – even thematizing notions of return within them. But he doesn't leave it at that. So keen is he to stay within the ambit of the tradition that he will not just pen 'original' poems but devote substantial effort to translating that tradition's finest products. Translation lies among the most effective forms of fidelity, and Pound worked at it tirelessly – even though translation, more yet than preservation, constitutes a supplement and therefore a threat to the tradition's integrity.

In the light of which, the fact that T. S. Eliot didn't produce translations as such appears significant. Yes, Eliot's poems 'translate' the tradition they inherit, in the sense that they are highly allusive, but contrary to Pound, Eliot appraises the tradition and very much wishes to add to it (the fact that Pound cut Eliot's draft of *The Waste Land* seems telling in this regard). No anxiety about excess will dog him in the way it did his colleague, because Eliot thinks of tradition as unfinished. In fact, the tradition has to be viewed as unfinished or else there is no room for new poets to continue it. Not preservation but prolongation is his métier.

To Eliot the tradition becomes a place, a location, of the kind celebrated in *Four Quartets*, where villages can be returned to and one can resume worship on the site. One kneels down on the poetic tradition and recites one's prayer in a way that is validated by the prayers that have been enounced on the same spot for centuries. The modern(ist) poem should posit itself where poetry has gone before, and take up the saying in an idiom which incorporates the old but expresses itself in the language of the new. This is what the poem is: a place of accretion. It stands in a space where poems have stood before, and being located in this way allows it to channel ancient voices which are then inflected through the voice box of the incoming poet and spoken as modern. Which suggests that the words in a poem are chambers of resonance; they cannot be used to close down on the thing they signify, because they are not flat, but long; they listen as much as speak.

Two qualifications, however. 'Burnt Norton' proposes that 'If all time is eternally present/ All time is unredeemable'.[7] According to this logic, Eliot would want to resist tradition on the grounds that it amounts to an eternal present – the pervasive presence of the past. In which case, the poem should actually avoid becoming a site of accretion, as that would make redemption impossible: remember that according to Eliot's Christianity redemption ranks among the greatest goods, and there is no redemption if you can't go back. But that is too glib a reading. It is in Pound rather than in Eliot that all time is eternally present, because Pound wants the past to be preserved in a way that defies time by definition. Eliot, by contrast, is committed to history as the accumulation of events, especially where those events occur in the same place. The poem as accretion is what allows for the diachrony of history, the staggering of time, the filing of poetical moments in chronological order, which in turn allow for redemption.

The second qualification is that although in Eliot the poetic word listens, it doesn't listen to everything. When it tunes into 'the tradition', it does so in a highly selective way that favours literature which is conservative, royalist, Anglo-Catholic, and so on.[8] Eliot's revisionism is blatant, and the modern poem serves ideological as well as aesthetic ends. That makes disputing the canon Eliot assembles easy: harder is to challenge the notion that all traditions are selective. Is it not axiomatic, in fact, that a tradition isn't everything? Involving the restricted transfer of values, tradition is no synonym for the past but a cut-out from it; tradition is the vector through which the past becomes private, or at least restricted, in the sense of being appropriated and made to mean something for a particular demographic. And so with the emergence of a tradition arrives a set of criteria by which this or that poet can be admitted; those that are accrue a certain mystery. All of which suggests a further point, that a preoccupation with tradition is highly compatible with a preoccupation with the esoteric. The ineffability that mesmerized the Eliot of the hyacinth and rose gardens fits well with his insistence on a specific line through poetic history, for at the centre both are closed.

That closedness is dense, dense with the codes of the tradition, like the folded petals of the rose in the garden. Into its whorl are gathered the tradition's symbols – like Dante's rose – as well as the modern, private meanings contributed to the symbol by the new poet – Eliot's rose as the lock that opens into a place of redemption that is never guaranteed. But once posited by the new poet, the rose (in this case) passes back out to circulate within the tradition's restricted economy. The symbol in a poetic genealogy is like a gene in a biological one, encrypting information from the past and to some degree limiting variants in the future; it is an image with a highly determined meaning. This makes the tradition in poetry as much a parade of the coded images that we call symbols as a procession of the personalities or even the works of its poets. It also reinforces the notion of the poem as autobiographical – for the symbol must be appropriated and made private, its meaning extracted and adapted, in order to produce a renovated, meaningful image capable of acquiring symbolic resonance. The image is first and foremost the language in which the poem speaks to itself.

Excess

This denseness of the image, especially when it has amassed meaning through its symbolic use by previous poets, points to a classic topos in poetic theory, namely that the poem *exceeds* itself – not just through images that have taken on the profound subjectivity I'm describing, but through the excess beauty we glimpsed in Pound, and so on. This excess – and it's a word I have used several times in the chapter – plays off against the poem's formal concision and cleanness, so that, schematically at least, the poem does the inverse of what the novel, with its formal open-endedness and exegetic approach to meaning, tends to do. A poem is a container for the uncontainable, and I want now to move on from the notion of tradition to this second 'line' through modern poetic theory, the trait of excess.

I say 'modern' poetic theory even though I've just conceded that 'excess' is a classic topos. What's distinct about modern concepts of the poem as formal excess, as containing the uncontainable, is that they tend to break away from the sublime. Wordsworth's *The Prelude*, for example, is excessive in the sense that the experience it describes in certain passages outflanks the poet's cognition; what he records is a non-cognitive impression, an overwhelming of the faculty of judgement, and is all the more poetic for being so. Modern poetic excess stays less on the side of the author, more on the side of the text, as a surplus within the poem. This can be the case in even the simplest of poetry:

A Picture

A little
house with
small
   windows,

    a gentle
    fall of the
    ground to
    a small

stream. The trees
are both close
and green, a tall
sense of enclosure.

There is a sky
of blue
and a faint sun
through clouds.

The poem is by Robert Creeley and it is hard to think of anything
more 'naive' (on the back cover of my edition, John Ashbery is
quoted as saying Creeley's poetry is 'basic').[9] Of course there is a
tradition of naive art that lends the poem a modicum of aesthetic
depth; and the fact that the poem concerns a picture means its
relationship with the vernacular reality it purports to depict
includes a complicating fold. Still, the poem can hardly be said to
contain the uncontainable – with the exception, that is, of 'a tall/
sense of enclosure'. The phrase describes a sense that doesn't make
sense. How can a sense be tall? We take it to refer back to the trees
that are visually tall, perhaps, but then the poem craftily transfers
the tallness of the trees to a sense. What does it mean? We might
misread the phrase to understand 'a sense of tall enclosure', because
we can picture a tall enclosure. Or just as we might lazily speak of
'a dramatic sense' instead of 'sense of drama', we can take 'a tall
sense' simply to mean 'a sense of the tall'. Alternatively, the poem
might be performing hypnosis on us, the reader, whereby we come
to believe our senses can indeed vary in height, and that in this
case they're tall, possibly out of supernatural sympathy with the
trees. There could even be an element of the sublime – something
is cognitively awry – if it were not that that miscognition owes not
to a sublime experience of the Wordsworthian ilk, which throws
the poet outside of himself, but to the brute juxtaposition of the
word 'tall' with the word 'sense', which is right for the context but
wrong for the meaning.

I do not claim this is how all modern excess works, except in
so far as modernity licenses itself to include in its poetry phrases
that don't stack up. Not that 'tall sense' creates a purely cognitive
challenge: it is what you might call a beautiful mistake, a logical
error that produces unintended beauty. The cognitive liability

makes way for an aesthetic asset. Because for all its plainness, Creeley's poem does, in this almost unimaginable image of a tall sense of enclosure surrounded by trees, feature an unanticipated thickening of its fabric. The otherwise smooth plane of the text suddenly gains some texture to stand proud of it, which cannot quite be rubbed back into the grain of the poem. As such, this extra texture or extra-text represents that moment in its verses to which the poem might most credibly ascribe its poetical status. The paradox being that if this moment of excess is what best identifies the poem as poetic, the poem realizes its identity outside itself.

Alternative articulations in literary criticism of the excess topos are not hard to come by, and I shall quickly cite three. This from R. P. Blackmur's *Language as Gesture* of 1952:[10]

> Gesture, in language, is the outward and dramatic play of inward and imaged meaning. It is that play of meaningfulness among words which cannot be defined in the formulas of the dictionary, but which is defined in their use together; gesture is that meaningfulness which is moving, in every sense of that word: what moves the word and what moves us.

Blackmur's is an account of synergy, of the inter-animation of the parts of a text that produces a 'gesture' greater than their sum. That word 'gesture', along with 'dramatic' and 'play' (twice), plus 'moves' (also twice) and 'moving' all avert to the theatrical, and to the theatrical as an environment in which affect smothers cognition. Or rather, the poet achieves 'meaningfulness', which is a ravishing plenitude of sense whereby sense is nevertheless surpassed by something highly emotional. For leverage, Blackmur takes a cheap shot at what is 'defined in the formulas of the dictionary', and in so doing makes a furtive claim for the superiority of art over science. Poetry, theatre, art belong in one affective nexus. What is the affect in question? It seems Blackmur envisions a cumulative, incantatory power whereby language leads both producer and consumer into an altered state – a late version of the sublime, perhaps. A beautiful distortion or sentimental disfiguring occurs whereby 'the poet is likely to make his purest though not his profoundest gestures when most beside himself'. The excess of sense tips over into inspired madness or rapt self-othering, and the result is the most fluent gesture, the most poetic poem.

Behind Blackmur's account of poetic excess, a poet idol seems to stand, a figure with a creative, searching and thespian sensibility, whose poems form part of a psychological project with a somewhat Nietzschean flavour. This psychologistic approach to poetry can be instructively contrasted with that in a text published three years later by Donald Davie, called *Articulate Energy*, whose emphasis lies more on a poem's linguistics. (The battle between psychological and linguistic criticism constitutes a topos of its own. Think of the argument between Harold Bloom and Paul de Man, the former insisting on literature's foundation in the psyche of the author, the latter at pains to prove literature's fundamentally rhetorical character, whereby psychological depth is an illusion created by a text's tropes.) For Donald Davie the poem's excess – what, following Bergson, he calls an 'intensive manifold' – squeezes out through its syntax. Davie writes that

> Syntax assists explanation, but explanation is unfolding, and intensive manifolds, which should be poetry's main concern, cannot be unfolded; hence it appears that syntax is out of place in poetry.[11]

In this contrast between syntactic unfolding and poetic enfolding there might be an analogue with my own dyad of narrative and image. Like syntax, narrative holds an 'explanatory' power; like enfolding, the image constitutes a quasi-cryptic density that stops the poem spinning in order to lead us through a wormhole into its centre. Equally, the phrase 'intensive manifolds', meant to refer to T. E. Hulme though also evoking Kant's 'manifold of apperception', might bring to mind again the image of a rose as being not only a poetic symbol, but a symbol of the poem as colour concentrated into beguiling pleats. That said, Davie's language in the quote above steers closer to the epistemological than the aesthetic, making poetic excess a challenge to knowledge more than an invitation to admire the poem's beauty.

My final example of the topos of excess comes from William Empson, for whom the reason why a poem adds up to more than the sum of its parts is hermeneutic complexity. Poems are incorrigibly ambiguous, and Empson famously and indefatigably catalogues ambiguity's seven types. In the manner of a logical positivist, he construes poetry as an extreme language of information, so if alongside Davie you should read Bergson, the text to go with Empson is Wittgenstein. Indeed Empson refers to a 'belief that all sorts of poetry may be conceived as explicable', and his admirable analyses refuse to yield to any final inexplicability on the poem's part. Which means a poem does in fact add up to the sum of its parts, without remainder, even if the same poem can equal different amounts, depending on the number of ambiguities it scores.

Before going on to poetry, Empson opens by discussing an avowedly unpoetic cat on a mat, and this movement from the plain to the fancy suggests that ambiguity occurs post-facto, befalling an ideally simple and original information-bearing statement. This would position poetry as a state of ongoing linguistic accident and impurity, and the poem as a stone gathering the moss of ambiguity around an otherwise hard and lucid middle. But what if poetry were ambiguous a priori rather than a posteriori? What if its excess derived not from the extra or double meanings it generates, but from an inherent obliquity? I am thinking here of Veronica Forrest-Thompson's 'non-meaningful levels of language'. Although displaying its own Empsonian affection for poetic taxonomies, her book *Poetic Artifice* makes the bold claim that 'the poem is always different from the utterances it includes or imitates'.[12] She is almost saying that the poem has an essence, extra to its utterances, where its truth resides. Almost, because that would be a Platonic gesture. Her use of the word 'different' sucks the transcendental afflatus out of such a claim, while retaining some of its mystery. Empson would perhaps bridle at that, and yet his own concept of 'diffuseness' – especially as manifested in Sidney's *Arcadia* – offers something not incompatible. Although due largely to its monotony, Sidney's poem, in Empson's reading of it, slowly sends out a kind of smoke in which the poem's technique, otherwise so showy, gets unaccountably obscured.[13] The smoke is the poem, its own excess, the result rather than the operation of its literary devices. It leaves an excess of sorts, an aftermath that begins at the beginning, an atmosphere that accompanies the text and makes it 'different' from its utterances. But perhaps that is just *Arcadia*: diffuseness spreading much to other texts may not be very likely.

Language and being

The notion of an excess in poetry is something of a fetish. It turns the poem into a bewitching object, as if the criticism that insists upon it were either superstition or displaced theology. But nor is the attempt to account for poetry in purely materialist terms ever satisfactory. If 'poetic' signals anything distinctive, it is a limit to cognitive apprehension. After all, what lies beyond that limit describes the field of most poetic theory: Is it where poetry ascends into the sublime? Withdraws into otherness? Transforms itself into music? In contrast, say, to eighteenth-century sentiment, which is broadly content for poetry to be intellectually diverting and/or morally instructive, modernity demands something altogether less useful: it wants poems to be meaningful for the individual reader, especially where meaning both presents and conceals itself, both gratifies and provokes that reader's interpretative hunger.

In this context, Heidegger's theory of poetry occupies an especially interesting place. Before he arrives at it, however, there is a long run-up, which involves systematically replacing the overly technical terms of Latin-based Western philosophy with modern revisions of the original Greek thinking it too officiously buries. In particular, he wants to get rid of instrumentalist concepts of existence in favour of Being, which stands at the origin of everything. But by his mid-career, Heidegger comes to see Being itself less as the master-concept it always threatens to look like – because that would be to repeat the Latin mistake of deploying an instrumental terminology to describe a world that is only slightly instrumental – and more as a term that must always be calibrated with other terms, and in particular 'language', which becomes virtually coterminous with it.

Being and language, language and Being – these form the interdependent pillars of some of Heidegger's most interesting texts, and their union shows itself most effectively in poetry; with its specially attentive relationship to language, poetry enjoys a privileged relationship to Being. It is that idiom in which Being speaks most effectively, and Heidegger will provide readings of Hölderlin, Trakl, Rilke and so on, in order to prove his point.[14] In its capacity as Being's most excellent sayer, poetry surpasses the poet. Language speaks, says Heidegger famously. According to a topos even more entrenched than that of excess, which goes back to the figure of the Aeolian harp, the poet becomes less an 'author' than the secretary of a more potent potency that speaks through him. He vibrates with Being, without ever being quite in control of it, while the poem itself, though never an aesthetic object in any ordinary sense, continues its archaic, ontic drone in a way that should be compelling for anyone with ears to hear.

But the somewhat dogmatic assertion of Being, and of the poem as Being's mouthpiece, might represent a fetish of its own. Paul de Man, for example, is highly suspicious of such Heideggerianism in the context of poetry because it seems to avoid poetry's (and language's) essentially rhetorical character. One can interpret 'Being' as a Platonistic idealization, and the edifice of Heideggerian ontology as the last bastion of the metaphysics Heidegger believed he was escaping. Equally, it can be read as the attribution to the poem of a sacred character which modernity has suppressed – a form of the 'displaced theology' I mentioned above. Besides, Heidegger's emphasis on German poetry seems to be working to a nationalist agenda.

So one way of testing the notion of the poem as the language of Being might be to look at a poem in English, a language striking for its genetic impurity, and a poem that seems devoid of Heideggerian baggage. This is Derek Walcott's 'Midsummer, Tobago':[15]

Broad sun-stoned beaches.

White heat.
A green river.

A bridge,
scorched yellow palms

from the summer-sleeping house
drowsing through August.

Days I have held,
days I have lost,

days that outgrow, like daughters,
my harbouring arms.

Is this the language of Being? It is unlikely Walcott has much Heideggerian theory in mind, and at first sight the poem doesn't fit with it. Far from language speaking through the poet, the poet seems in control of the language, and the subject matter appears to be a personal reflection brought about by a scene in Tobago, not far from Walcott's native St Lucia; the use of the first person pronoun erects a particular barrier to the entry of impersonal Being.

That said, any reader of Heidegger could seize the word 'bridge' and recall the philosopher's meditation on it: 'The bridge *gathers* to itself in *its own* way earth and sky, divinities and mortals.'[16] To Heidegger, the bridge is a place of connection that allows what he calls the 'fourfold' of earth, sky, divinities and mortals to come together, and thereby affirm the ontic character of the world. So is it too much to bridge from Heidegger's to Walcott's bridge?

The bridge in the poem has an important relationship to time as the passing of days, and the medium in which the daughters grow, while itself being highly 'located'. The poem as a whole operates by putting time and place in tension with one another, a tension that begins with the title 'Midsummer, Tobago', two coordinates intersecting to create a singularity. For Heidegger, this singularity of location is important: put simply, place comes before the idea of place, and its singularity lies in the fact that it is stronger than any idea of it. It seems borne out by the Walcott, in which we are given not the idea of a bridge, but a specific bridge in Tobago in midsummer as witnessed, one assumes, by the poet himself. The poem insists on a 'there and then' and on the impossibility of substituting the specifics of the image for something else.

Such specifics would seem to be owned by the speaker in the poem – the experience is his, and his sense-impressions are necessary for the specifics to impress themselves as such. The poem doesn't just combine a time and a place, but a time and a place *for a certain person*, the speaker in the poem. It could be filed under 'identity moderne' were it not for the poem's theme of losing experience, of not being able to retain it. 'Days I have held' is quickly succeeded by 'days I have lost', and the sequence gathers to a falling climax with 'days that outgrow [...] my harbouring arms'. The fixity of the sense-impressions meets an image-solvent whereby what is remembered is the forgetting, and the speaker is flummoxed by what passes by or beyond him, what he can no longer harbour. Could this be the language of Being speaking through Walcott, its hapless vessel?

Whatever the answer, a second concept of time has now entered the poem. The first was that of the moment of midsummer; this is of time as transience, exhibited by the growth of daughters and the implicit ageing of their father. The speaker occupies a place in a schema of the generations in which 'mortals', to use Heidegger's word, have to pass on and are replaced by their children. 'Midsummer', on this account, stands for a mid-point in life, a noonday as hot as the 'White heat', that has ticked over towards an evening, and made the speaker recall his mortality even as he starts to forget the 'days' which are the counters of biological life. The bridge over the river prompts this intimation of mortality; in Heideggerian terms it allows human beings to be gathered into their Being-towards-death.

Clearly, people exist in genealogies, but do poems and the theories about them? I have tried in this chapter to trace a few lines suggesting where the DNA might be shared. I have also given weight to the idea that owing to its equivocal relationship to narrative, the poem balks at such classification, and it is on this note that I wish to conclude. Reading 'Midsummer, Tobago' again, I realize that something is missing. While time and place are so heavily scored, these two dimensions remain strangely unaccompanied by a necessary third – an event. Nothing happens, and the poem's first half reads like the prose set-up of a film script, before the point where the dialogue ought to cut in:

Broad sun-stoned beaches.

White heat.
A green river.

A bridge,
scorched yellow palms

from the summer-sleeping house
drowsing through August.

Later we have 'days that outgrow', where outgrowing denotes an action, but days are the platform for events, not the events themselves. Ditto the days held and lost, which are event-shells rather than the stories they might have encased. And just where, after the word 'August', one expects a narrative intervention, a character, a word, or a movement, one is deprived of it; the reader loses the day of the poem that they expected to hold, as if in parallel process with the speaker's own loss. This somewhat eerie privation, the harbour that no longer welcomes in the arrival of the event, seems to me emblematic of the poem –which chooses to keep drowsing rather than wake up to any reality.

2

Rhyme and reason

Is poetry rational? Is poetry reasonable? Is rhyme rational? Is rhyme reasonable? Does reason rhyme? Is rhyme a kind of non-reason, or nonsense?

It is readily accepted among today's cultural elite that modern poetry doesn't have to rhyme – as if it is an unreasonable demand to be so reasonably rhyming in an age where, in the face of individualism and self-expression, reason has been agreed to have surrendered much of its universalizing dominance. Effects of continuity and wholeness, such as rhyme produces, no longer equate to rational poetic decorum as they might have done, say, for Alexander Pope: they have become spurious in their outmodedness, and childish in their results. The connections made between rhyming words seem adventitious, so if you must write a rhyming poem, better make the rhymes as deft as possible. True, not rhyming leaves you open to the charge that, like an abstract painter who avoids figurative art, you simply lack the technical ability to carry off this traditional craft. But because that craft looks to modern eyes so very contrived, being against rhyme in modern poetry carries the more sympathetic rationale.

Two oddities follow. First, modern free verse needs a rationale to justify its rejection of the reasonableness of rhyme, even though its freeness ought to mean it doesn't need to justify itself at all. Second, that freedom is further curbed by singling out one poetic technique (rhyming) as off-limits, where all others are admissible. Rhyme operates as a cordon sanitaire around modern free verse, substituting a negative rule (Don't rhyme!) for the positive rule (Do rhyme!) it formerly imposed. The spectre of rhyme still patrols the poem's boundaries.

And yet the orderliness of rhyme never had much reason to begin with. Far more delinquent than it appears, rhyme might even represent a precious resource to the modern poet keen to depart from the main. How so? Rhyme qua rhyme is the simple matching of words according to how they sound and/or look; a rhyme is a rhyme whether or not any semantic connection links the relevant words. 'Table' and 'fable' meet all the criteria needed for rhyming; that there's little or no connection between the words at the level of meaning matters not. A rhyme is a rhyme regardless of whether one can infer semantic links between elements rhymed, and so it possesses an aleatory superficiality that might appeal to the modern, or at least the modernist, sensibility, especially as the latter manifests itself in, say, surrealism or Dada. Strictly speaking, rhyme is nonsense.

It is around this nonsensical core that the rhyming bard hopes to weave a plausible semantic structure, made up of the threads of the two or more matching words. Thus I could manipulate 'table' and 'fable', apparently so little connected, to produce the following couplet:

> Engraved upon the mythic table,
> The knights read of the coming fable.

I accept the poetry is undistinguished, but it at least forces 'table' and 'fable' into a passingly meaningful relationship with each another, based on an allusion to the Round Table. The fact it is an allusion that helps the rhyme to make sense is important, because it suggests that the 'meaning' achieved by rhyming words lies not in the words themselves but the context in which they are stationed. One can picture rhyming words as stars put into attraction with one another by the gravity produced by surrounding words. On their own, 'table' and 'fable' still fail to make sense; only when the words around them are appended do 'table' and 'fable' begin to relate to one another, even as the rhyme per se is neither improved nor impaired in the new context.

Not that it is only the context within a poem that helps the rhyme falsely appear meaningful. Say I change the couplet to:

Snow falls. Inside, a kitchen table.
A plane flies on to France. A fable.

This time I have tried to do the reverse. Instead of using the antecedent terms to help the rhyming words make sense in relation to each other, I have put in a series of disconnected images, hoping now to separate 'table' and 'fable' from one another, and expose more of the rhyme's inner nonsense. But my attempt is not entirely successful, because now you, the reader, are likely to fill the semantic vacuum that has been created. You will want to frame the couplet in such a way that it does make a kind of sense to you. To be sure, it doesn't take a rhyming couplet to stimulate a reader's hermeneutic instinct to make sense of a poem, but the rhyme does emphasize to the reader that sense is there to be made. This time the meaning of the two-line poem will lie more in the head of the reader than in the lines that lead up to each rhyming word, though it doesn't change the fact that the rhyme as such is meaningless.

As I said, this intrinsic meaninglessness of rhyme, its nonsense factor, ought to be more attractive than it is to a modern mindset: it would seem to play to the subversive instincts of surrealism. And in the verse of, say, Edward Lear, which is expressly 'nonsense verse', it does – but this is perhaps the problem. Modern poetry in general, or specifically its more modernist modes, will not embrace rhyme even in its self-consciously nonsensical mode, because the latter risks looking like comedy, and this offends modern(ist) poetry's taste for seriousness – which includes the longing for meaning, especially at the personal level. Modern free verse exists much more to serve this personal need than that of a synthetic or subversive aesthetic as encapsulated in nonsensical rhyme.

This play between meaning and its opposite, already written into rhyming poetry, becomes highly exposed in the first verse of Robert Lowell's 'Waking Early Sunday Morning':[1]

O to break loose, like the chinook
salmon jumping and falling back,
nosing up to the impossible
stone and bone-crushing waterfall—
raw-jawed, weak-fleshed there, stopped by ten
steps of the roaring ladder, and then

to clear the top on the last try,
alive enough to spawn and die.

Pleasingly, the rhyme achieves greater and greater resolution as
the salmon make their own connection, from 'chinook' rhyming
rather obliquely with 'back' in the first lines, to the more complete
'try' and die' in the last. Lowell uses the incremental increase in the
matching of the end-words in each couplet to represent the salmon's
faltering leaps towards success. But the representation between
poem and salmon flips both ways, inserting a self-referential
mirror in among the verse, glinting like the silver flanks of the fish.
Once the rhyme fully realizes itself, the verse dies, as if it, like a
salmon, has consummated its own meaningfulness and can pass
on to the next stanza; the poem is about the effort to make rhyme
meaningful, using salmon as an image of itself. Yes, the fact that
rhyme is essentially meaningless drives a counter-current against
reason, gushing all the while against semantic connections. At last,
however, comes the leap of faith by which 'try' and 'die' connect
meaningfully on their own terms: 'in life, one is trying to die, to
secure the life of those that come after', or something like that.

Which is all fine, except a poem that draws so much attention to
its own rhyme scheme not only threatens to subvert itself, looking
more artificial and less meaningful as each couplet clicks by; it also
pricks up our ears to 'rhymes' where they're not supposed to exist,
right down to the absurd, *de minimis* examples: every 'the' in the
poem is, strictly speaking, a rhyme with every other 'the'; and the
same with the word 'to'. Unless, that is, a rhyme differs from a
repetition, in which case 'table' and 'fable' makes a rhyme where
'table' and 'table' doesn't. A rhyme requires the back end of the two
words to be the same, but the front end to vary. Though internal
rhymes can and do exist, this whole-word rule is what generally
dissuades us from breaking poems down to smaller units whereby
letters in individual words could rhyme with the same letter in any
other word. Conversely, rhyme should not operate with units larger
than the word, because a rhyming *phrase,* in which all the words
in a sequence match all the words in a previous sequence in order,
would be something else altogether. Here is another I have made up:

Days come. Days go.
Plays dumb. Says no.

Again, one can dress the lines up with semantic trappings, and so make them mean something. After all, the complete repetition in line 2 of the sounds from line 1 seems to reinforce the poem's 'theme' of a circular pointlessness. But we would still say the rhyme as such belongs with 'go' and 'no'.

And if the rhyme belongs with the end-words, it means rhyme cannot be separated from rhythm. There is 'nosing' in line 3 and 'roaring' in line 6 of the Lowell above; 'break' in line 1 and 'weak' in the 'weak-fleshed' in line 5; and so on. All are whole words in their own right, and all 'rhyme' in a certain sense. But what prevents them from rhyming properly is where they have been placed. The gratification that comes with rhyme has to do with more than semantic connection; the fact the gratification is both expected and deferred gives a rhyme its special quality, and to such an extent that gratification and semantics, meaning and pleasure, cannot be so easily divorced. So how do we account for this phenomenon, that rhyme, which is hollow of meaning, even nonsensical, is nevertheless capable of generating meaning and pleasure to the point of their being interfused, over and above any meaning already generated by the surrounding words and/or the interpretative projections of its reader?

Rhyme appears to be a device which, when coupled with rhythm, seems like Lowell's salmon to jump the meaninglessness barrier. I say 'when coupled with rhythm', but rhyme without rhythm isn't rhyme either:

Letter.
Better.

That's a two-line poem in which the words rhyme and yet there is no substantive rhyming to speak of (like 'table' and 'fable' earlier). Once more, an arbitrariness in rhyme has been exposed – or rather, the fact that rhyme is purely visual and/or phonic becomes painfully evident. But as soon as we add in some rhythm, we shift into an extra dimension:

He plans to write a humble letter.
A phone call would be so much better.

We haven't just added in rhythm, of course: we have added words that mark that rhythm, and with those words comes an entire apparatus of meaning, even on this miniature scale. Most apparent is the narrative scene and the 'meaning' that comes with that, in the form of our speculations about the man's psychology, who he is writing to, the back story, and so on. On top of the narrative, however – or underneath it – we have the original rhyme (letter/ better) along with a rhythm considered as a pattern of beats (two lots of four iambs, each with a soft ending in an extra beat). How do they work together, and in what sense do they create any meaning extra to that we can extract thanks to our interpretations? A rhyme is not intrinsic to the narrative, so in what sense can it contribute to any kind of meaning, especially as it is semantically null?

The first point to underscore is that, in poetry at least, rhyme without rhythm isn't rhyme; it is just a list of words that match. Rhyme is a rhythmic matching, and rhythm can't work without temporalization and spatialization, which are effectively the same. Rhythm s/paces out the words in a poem in a pattern; when that pattern incorporates words at the end of two or more lines that match, the rhythmic poem rhymes. And so, by slotting the matching words into the end of certain lines, rhythm controls the profligacy of rhyme. It tells us which words are to be taken as matching – those at the end of the line – and to ignore matches that pop up elsewhere (let's set aside internal rhymes for now). It maps the architecture of the poem in terms of where the weight is distributed; and because rhyme/rhythm operate on patterns, the distribution is typically regular.

Whence the second order 'meaning' that the rhyming poem achieves. I put meaning in quotation marks because the meaning that results from rhythm has less to do with semantic content than with that sense of architectural distribution. The poem becomes meaningful in so far as it has followed architectural convention, planting words according to a template or pro forma that is meaningful mainly by virtue of its recognizability. If, however, 'meaning' is not the right word, this familiar rightness could just as well be termed 'rationality', on the grounds that the rhyming/ rhythmic architecture works on a sense of ratio so central to (as least classical notions of) reason. Despite the nonsense that infects it, rhyme, when put into order by rhythm, reacquires the orderly proportion that one associates with reason as the harmonious ratio of elements.

Whence also the inclusion of gratification and pleasure. Though modernity has played its part in driving a wedge between pleasure and reason, to the point of setting them up as adversaries, the two are not so easily decoupled. The harmonious, rational distribution of rhyming elements in a poem is pleasing because a harmonious, rational distribution of rhyming elements is pleasing. And if in the previous paragraph I too hastily slid from 'meaning' to 'reason', meaning still has its place in this pleasurable conjuncture. When a poem rhymes, and specifically when a line rhymes, it hands over a certain yield that had been promised in the words leading up to it. Regardless of content, this yield, this moment of reward best describes what meaning is as affect. Meaning is the feeling of reward. It might get converted by a reader into meanings pertinent to him or her – such is the labour of interpretation – but the meaning of a given rhyme lies more fundamentally in its rewarding that reader with a sense of good closure. Meaning and rhyme have an affinity in their capacity to reward readers with a completeness, no matter how temporary.

Lowell's poem continues, now in Wordsworthian fashion, as follows:

Stop, back off. The salmon breaks
water, and now my body wakes
to feel the unpolluted joy
and criminal leisure of a boy—
no rainbow smashing a dry fly
in the white run is free as I,
here squatting like a dragon on
time's hoard before the day's begun!

All the anxiety of rhyming, all the anticipatory jumps toward closer identity in the first stanza, are now steadied with a set of more unalloyed rhymes (though 'dragon on' and 'day's begun' are hardly felicitous). But in tandem with this more innocuous pleasure of rhyme, we get the guilt, as Lowell rewards himself with it at his own 'criminal leisure'. Why would rhyming represent a guilty pleasure? Not just because it operates as reward, as 'time's hoard', that deferred quantum now ready for the taking. The problem with rhyme is that it cannot disguise how patently language serves as a resource available to all and sundry. There is little private genius involved in working through a list of words to see which ones will fit a rhyme in your poem, because that list already exists out there, as fixed and accessible as a set of numbers. Even the poet, notable for his or her gifts in subduing language to private – or at least restricted – meaning, will have few means of expanding this hoard. On the contrary, the fact that rhyming words are so limited removes a significant burden of invention from the poet and, with it, a portion of the poet's claim to complete inventiveness. When in conjunction with rhythm, rhyme s/paces out words in a line, for the sake of a rewarding meaning delivered at that line's end. It does so with a view to a pre-existent 'hoard' of rhyming words – a hoard that was always already there, 'squatting like a dragon on/ time's hoard before the day's begun!'. That dragon serves as an emblem of rhyme. What is deferred is not what is to come, according to the poem's private agenda of withholding the rhyming word until the right moment, but what had previously accumulated in the public domain, belonging to no one in particular. The poet's deferring of a matching word suggests she or he owns it, but this is not the case; a rhymed poem is even more conspicuously an 'open-source' text than any other. And so that deferral is disingenuous, and the lack of the matching word in the line leading up to it is not a lack but a veiled presence.

In a sense, of course, all deferral is the deferral of the past rather than the future. There has to be something there to be deferred – in this case, a matching word housed in a public storage facility, borrowed by the poet then concealed from the reader until the point in the poem where the rhythm demands it be revealed. It is a notion that resonates with Freud's concept of delayed action or *Nachträglichkeit* or 'deferred action',[2] and much of what I have been discussing could be elaborated in psychoanalytic terms, especially in relation to the Lowell poem, where in that first stanza the deferment has to do with the deferment of spawning, and the anguish of fertility flashing in the sexual and philoprogenitive image of the salmon. Generally speaking, rhythm serves as a moderating force on the pleasures of rhyme, a superegoic function relative to the egoic reward that comes when two words match. In so far as rhyme has to do with deferment it is a question of libidinal control; pleasure 'exists' only as the deferment of itself, or rhythm in other words. Its moment of release is one of both reduction (death) and production (genitivity), so it is not strictly speaking a

moment of pleasure, for pleasure is diverted to both sides of it –
killed on the one hand, and superseded on the other. Having only
deferred itself, when it comes to it the moment of pleasure is not
a moment of pleasure, but the moment of pleasure dividing. The
rhyme completes itself and dies, while also emerging, fertilized, in
a filial form.

What about cases where the rhythm is more complex, and
doesn't deliver the rhyme quite at the anticipated moment?

> Let us go then, you and I
> When the evening is spread out against the sky
> Like a patient etherised upon a table.[3]

'The Love Song of J. Alfred Prufrock' features a series of jazz rhythms
that toy with readers' expectations. Here the word 'sky' rhymes
with 'I', but does so nearly too late, attenuating the gratification
it could have provided earlier and more straightforwardly. The
words 'spread out' in line 2 do double service in both naming and
effecting a spreading out of the line from four to five beats (or more,
depending how you read it). The extra foot makes the sky seem
further out and higher up; like the rhyme it is only just graspable.
The reaching then falls flat in the third line upon the bathetic 'table'
that, lacking a matching word in the next line that would make it
the first half of a second couplet, just stands there. This serves to
'etherize' the reader's own sentiments, as if, like the Lowell poem,
the text seems to be discussing itself in parallel with its ostensible
subject matter. In philosophy the table is the universal basic object,
that which is the most neutral thing in the world, prose rendered
into physical form. Here the table's refusal to rhyme, thus breaking
with the scheme only just instigated in the opening two lines, seems
especially insensitive – anaesthetized – to the poetic, in a way that
supports Eliot's wider drollery likening a romantic sky to a hospital
patient. This is where Freudian pleasure mutates into wit, where
bodily eros transforms into intellectual delight – the change that
Prufrock the character seeks to reverse on his quest to desublimate
the universe which he has both created from his mental materials
and been thrown into against his will.

'Prufrock' shuffles and dips along with a rhyme which, like
a drunk, sometimes slides out at the angles and loses its shape,
veering toward the free verse that was to supersede it. Relieved of

the exigencies that govern rhyme, unrhymed verse tunes instead
into the rhythm of inner necessities. Necessities of the inner variety
are necessary because external ones have receded, throwing the
unity of the free verse poem into question (assuming unity to be
one of its goals). How so? Most rhyming poems operate according
to a rhyme scheme that structures the poem throughout. Although
any such scheme can be repeated indefinitely, pointing towards its
poem's open-endedness, a given poem will finish upon the ending
of one of the scheme's cycles, like a piece of music ending on the
tonic rather than, say, the dominant, and it is this which establishes the poem's unity, its conforming with its own local rules. A
rhyming poem has to end because the rhyme scheme says so. With
unrhymed verse, the burden of ending lands on the poet who, if
the poem's unity is one of his or her aspirations, has to reach for
different levers. This produces the inescapable risk in unrhymed
poems of their 'finishedness' looking quite arbitrary. Why did it
stop there?

To some extent, the unrhymed poem can mitigate this effect, by
deploying other unifying effects, such as a motif, a repeated word
or a narrative progression from beginning to end. Alternatively, it
can resist the call for unity altogether, writing it off as arbitrary in
its own right, constraint for constraint's sake. Take the poem by
Charles Tomlinson, 'Drive':[4]

First light strikes
across a landmass
daylight hides: horizon
rides above horizon
momentarily
like a region of cloud:
I return driving
to the same view undone:
the windscreen takes it in
as a high and brilliant
emptiness that lies to one
of no depth, stretched above
palpabilities morning could touch:
and one feels for the features of the lost
continent (it seems)
of day's beginnings, recollection

seizing on the mind
with what infinity of unmarked
mornings, of spaces unsounded
habit abjures, in the cross-
tides of chaos, till we
believe our eyes (our lies)
that there is nothing there
but what we see—
and drive

I'm putting this up as an example of unrhymed verse, though there are some matching or semi-matching end words (not including the repetition of 'horizon'), dotted in: 'undone' and 'one', as well as 'we' and 'see' might deserve to be called rhymes, technically speaking; 'hides' and 'rides' is a sort-of internal rhyme, as is 'eyes (our lies)'. But by and large 'Drive' is an unrhymed poem, and its lack of rhyme scheme produces a ragged, incomplete feel. That is the lonesome drive of unrhymed verse, scrub and hot tundra along its verge. No doubt it is a choice that suits the subject 'Drive', which denotes progression without closure, an 'infinity of unmarked/ mornings'. It helps to create an existential mood; the 'unmarked' rhyme scheme chimes with the unmarked journey.

Tomlinson's poem projects a cinematographic silence around the edges of the lines, though the relationship to silence is not unique to 'Drive' – unrhymed poems tend to engage with silence in more nuanced ways than their rhymed equivalents. Here is a stanza I chose at random from Louis MacNeice's 'Half Truth from Cape Town':[5]

Between a smoking fire and a tolling bell
When I was young and at home I could not tell
What problems roosting ten miles to the west
Waited like vultures in their gantried nest
Till Prod should tumble Papish in the river.
I could not tell. The bell went on for ever.

The matching end-words fall like the *ding* of a typewriter at the end of the line; even where there's enjambment, a minimal and regular intake of breath is suggested, which keeps the poem to time. Compare it with some lines from the Tomlinson above:

I return driving
to the same view undone:
the windscreen takes it in
as a high and brilliant
emptiness that lies to one
of no depth, stretched above
palpabilities morning could touch:

The silence works in two directions. First, there is the semi-visual
silence as one line ends and the next begins, almost as if this
were prose. Secondly, the absence of a stable rhythm and the
near absence of punctuation takes each line into the whiter, more
expansive silence of the page or screen to its right, itself a kind
of 'high and brilliant/ emptiness'. The end-words resonate at an
uncertain frequency, and this gives the poem more than the casual
attitude of a lazy rhyme: it lends each line an almost psychological
depth. The analogy I would make is between perspective and
non-perspective in art. The rhymed poem works like the flat figures
in medieval stained glass, in that the poem's edges (the line endings)
emphasize form over character. The unrhymed poem allows each
line to develop a character of its own, regardless of any personages
portrayed in the poem, or any narrative voice it may contain; it
helps it to have a 'personality'. This personality speaks, and when
it stops speaking for the uncertain length of time at the end of the
line, opening up a variable silence, that variability makes for an
ambiguity which we the reader experience as momentary suspense.
We are challenged, in however fleeting a way, to engage with it, to
judge it, to feel uncertain by it.

   This sense of uncertainty, caused by the unevenness, the rippled
silence that we come across in unrhymed poems, throws us off
not only in the moment, but in retrospect. Put baldly, unrhymed
poetry is harder to remember, and one could make guesses about
the origins of rhymed poetry as having to rhyme because of its oral
nature. But rhymed poetry also remembers itself, in the sense that
the poet must conform to a pattern to be kept in mind; with each
new matching word, the poem recalls the one before, and if it is
set within a larger scheme, the poem keeps mirroring itself and so
develops a sense of 'who' it is. That is part of the unity I mentioned
above – an internal memory function. Lacking such a function,
the unrhymed poem puts itself more at risk. Though some brands

of literary criticism will seek out 'self-reference' in a text, the unrhymed poem, for all its self-referentiality in other respects, forgets itself in this specific sense of not having to remember a rhyme scheme, not having to occupy itself with itself in the same way. Just as a hard-to-measure silence tugs at its edges, so the lack of rhyme prises the poem that little further apart from itself. It is as if free verse is readier to say goodbye to itself, to be lost.

I have been hinting at wider connections between free verse and modernity. It is not just the rejection of traditional forms in the name of the poet's personal self-expression. Free verse represents modernity by opening up this gap in the relationship between the self and the self, the poem and the poem. Rather than confirming the poet's or the narrator's identity by pursuing an original (i.e. free) verse form, the lack of rhyme has an uncanny counter-effect. The poem doesn't close on itself in the same way and there is a subjectivity leak – a loss, rather than a gain, of the self. In Tomlinson's terms, drive becomes drift.

3

The object

I want to address poetic objects, particularly vases, urns, boxes, coffins, sarcophagi – objects that are more or less empty and upon which poetry fixes its fascinated attention. Such objects point to a relationship between poetry and death, but it is characteristic of poetry in general to flatter its object, regardless of whether that object is funereal. Such 'flattery' lies at the heart of poetic objectivity – a certain power of exclusion that leaves the object free in its 'objectal' state. One reason we find love poetry so exemplary of poetry is that it concerns an object whose exclusivity is so clear. The numberless ranks of the excluded serve to intensify the singularity of the beloved. Here, for instance, is Ted Hughes writing in 'A Pink Wool Knitted Dress' about Sylvia Plath on the day they were married:

> You were transfigured.
> So slender and new and naked,
> A nodding spray of wet lilac.
> You shook, you sobbed with joy, you were ocean depth
> Brimming with God.
> You said you saw the heavens open
> And show riches, ready to drop upon us.
> Levitated beside you, I stood subjected
> To a strange tense: the spellbound future.[1]

The word 'transfigured' captures well the objectal state of the object in poetry, in this case the bride. For a transfiguring is what

assists the object in coming before its viewer, washed with an
almost chemical visibility that lets it be seen in a privileged light,
even if that visibility can be blinding. Every object in poetry is
'transfigured' in the sense that it gets re-presenced for its beholder
and momentarily isolated from what encroaches; in some sense,
every poem aspires to report an epiphany. In this transfiguring,
a 'strange tense' emerges, for the object carves out its place of
permanence, binding it to the (spellbound) future. Objects in
poems are temporally spellbound because, having been transfigured
into a special presence for the poet, they simultaneously absent
themselves from that presence in order to stand forward in time,
in that future which will secure their longevity, making them an
object of memory. The object disappears into its future even as
it is beheld. The poem, in turn, constitutes a memorial for that
elective object, and the poet's bond with it that was already, like a
marriage vow, stretching outward into the future in the moment of
its being sealed. By the same token, the object averts to the poet's
mortality. Yes, he will live on through that object, but only in so
far as it becomes his monument: Keats' urn stands as a monument
to Keats. Alongside the mortality of the poet evoked by his chosen
object comes the apparent compensation that results from writing a
poem about it, in which both poem and object survive to comprise
the poet's legacy.

No doubt there are fetishistic or aggressive aspects to this positing
of the object by poems, and the Hughes poem could be taken to
task for a highly subjective framing of the woman figure represented by Plath (Hughes does write 'I stood subjected/ To a strange
tense'). In a not dissimilar vein, one could read the object in poetry
through a Kleinian lens, whereby each prized object symbolizes a
restorative, nostalgic love, associated with the maternal bond. To
write a poem about an object might be an exercise whereby the
poet seeks to have the mother as a loved object all to oneself: if I
choose a certain object this proves in turn how special I am, that I
am special to it. Common to both theories would be an assumption
about the object as in some sense 'female' – a 'chora', a vessel, or a
sounding-medium through which the typically male poet hopes his
voice will resonate.

For her part, Plath appears in some of her poetry all too
aware of her object status, particularly as it could be disaggre-
gated and abused either by others or by herself – for she is also

self-objectifying, even if she is so in order to pre-empt the objec-
tification perpetrated by others. When it comes to writing about
empty vessels of the more tangible kind, however – I'm thinking of
her bee-box – it too is significant for its ability to make sound:[2]

> I ordered this, this clean wood box
> Square as a chair and almost too heavy to lift.
> I would say it was the coffin of a midget
> Or a square baby
> Were there not such a din in it.

Again, the object seems to stand as an image of the poem
describing it – a square entity humming with dark sounds, often
scarcely intelligible, sometimes scary. But as much as the poem is
alive with bee-words, it is a dead object, almost in the Kleinian
sense. The speaker 'would say it was the coffin of a midget/ Or a
square baby', and from this we might infer psychotic proclivities
on the part of the speaker which have resulted in the 'murder' of
objects around her, rendering them as worthless as she perceives
herself to be. Except that the circus-like midget and square baby
are replaced by the 'din' of bees, and this causes the poem to skid
off the psychological landing-pad where it was about to alight –
especially because the word 'square' is repeated (or squared) as if to
establish the object's perimeters in such a way that no psychology,
no human mind, can get either in or out. The midgets and babies
usher us, as if in a theatre, toward psychological horrors, but then
the poem diverts us to the pure, somewhat automatic sound of the
box, whose din is so gloriously deplored. In so doing, the poem
averts to the box's ability to steal attention away from everything
else, despite the speaker's attempts to master it by asserting that
'They can be sent back'. In fact, the box, once posited by the
poem, remains, because it is never object enough; the bee-box
is the poem's aesthetic cousin, so to speak, a rival form, like a
sophisticated robot to the humanoid poem. Hence the heavy irony
of the poem's last line:

> The box is only temporary.

It is ironic because (a) the statement might be true, but it reads
like the speaker is in denial; (b) this is the last line of the poem,

and so it lingers, thus undoing or at least prolonging into time the 'temporary' status it denotes; (c) the box has by now been 'commemorated' by the poem anyway: even sending it back can't scratch out the memory of it as inscribed by the poem. What helps the box remain is that it was never simply 'there': it became not a symbol of Plath's mind, but an entity competing with the poem itself while forming a part of it, like an itch or – more appropriately – a sting. The box of bees is a sting on the poem's body.

The idea of sending the bee-box back forms a pair with the fact that the speaker ordered it in the first place. If she ordered it, it had to be summoned, meaning that its arrival was not inevitable. She was implicated in the choosing, and this notion of choosing the poetic object involves a necessary, if disconcerting, sense of the arbitrary. Klein's chief influence, Freud, speaks about choosing an object which is third in a sequence of three, and also a woman.[3] He explores the possibility of something inherently deathly about this number (and when Plath writes in 'Lady Lazarus' of her suicide attempts, she says with dark glee that 'This is Number Three').[4] Really it is little more than an intuition, but Freud tries to levy support for it from literature and myth: he talks for instance about *King Lear*, saying that Lear's 'choice', the acceptance-refusal, of the third daughter, Cordelia, is ostensibly a choice that would save him, whereas she presages death. It is another example of the human defaulting to death in the name of life, and compulsively so. The three sisters we already know, Freud says, from the Greeks: 'the Fates, the Moerae, the Parcae or the Norns, the third of whom is called Atropos, the inexorable'.[5] The third Fate is death, and out of pleasure, unwittingly, we always choose it. This is because the human psyche has two wires fatally crossed, the instinct for pleasure and the instinct for death: at the third stroke, we trigger the latter instead of the former. Freud's title, however, is 'The Theme of the Three Caskets', referring not to *King Lear* but *The Merchant of Venice*, and it is the fact that a casket so resembles a tomb which provides in part for the defunctive nature of the number three when it comes to picking the third casket (which also represents a woman – Portia). We can't help opting for the vessel we always wanted, the tomb-like home, or womb of being to which 'we' want to return.

Despite the hermetic significance that could be conjured up for the number three, I would suggest it is not the number per se that matters in the choosing of an object, but the choosing marking a point at which an otherwise endless series of numbers or choices is arrested. Three says stop, but other numbers say stop equally. (Jacques Derrida has an essay called 'Cartouches' which looks at miniature coffin-like objects created by an artist, whose series runs to the conspicuously random amount of 127.)[6] What seems to matter is less the particular number than an effect of seriality, along with the pre-eminence of a moment within a series, and the uncanny aura generated by anonymous selection. This event of selection implies death because it brings continuity to a standstill. It has little to do with the symbolic force of a given number, and more with the simple fact of choosing an object from a series, and thus stopping the spinning of the wheel of fortune. This object rather than that is chosen, and a certain closure takes place ... And if I refer to fortune, it is because something arbitrary must affect the choice of object, no matter how excellent the object appears. With every choice comes the knowledge that the object chosen could have been different; otherwise there wouldn't have been a choice. The 'transfiguring' of the object that goes on in a poem serves partly to mask this arbitrariness.

I talked in the Introduction about the distinction between the self-righting contingency of the novel and narrative, on the one hand, and the a-contingent hemming-in of poetic form, on the other. A poem tries to stop time, hence its profoundly non-pragmatic nature, and it does so chiefly through the image. Where narrative in poetry can be burned off, what is left are always the image-crystals. But what is the relationship between an image in a poem and an object that poem might address? Is Keats' urn an image or an object, or both? There is a relatively simple answer to this in linguistics: the image is the signified, the object the referent; there is the urn as pictured in the poem, and the urn of which the picture is a picture. But the simple answer needs to be complicated a little, because the image/signified itself takes on some 'objectal' status as a textual entity which outstays the poet in the manner I was describing a moment ago. Object and image to some degree bleed into one another, even if the textual object seems like a poor second best to the material reality of whatever urn it happened to be. The fact it's an urn seems apt, therefore, because an urn is an empty object; and when it's not empty, it's filled with ashes, which only represent another kind of absence. Like other vessels, the urn suggests both fullness and emptiness.

In short, the poem itself is a textual object that depicts real objects like urns, but those real objects are then manifested in the poem as images which endure and so achieve a quasi-objectal status of their own. What an ode to an object actually addresses therefore becomes rather difficult to say. Keats' poem addresses both a real urn and its own representation of that urn, but that representation forms part of the poem itself, thus warping its objectivity into something with the more subjective or apotropaic nature I tried to describe in the first chapter, in talking about poems as autobiographical. What is more, the urn, textual or real or both, is itself a container – it, like a poem, has content, even if the urn or the poem which addresses it never allows the content to be revealed, and so intimates that it could be hollow. In all cases, the reassuringly basic dyad of subject and object has to give way to a structure in which the relationships are harder to frame. This structure could perhaps take the shape of a Barbara Hepworth sculpture, in which a given form contains a hole. The hole is both part and not part of the piece, while it also makes a window onto what lies beyond in 'reality' (this reality usually being the space of an art gallery, which only complicates matters more).

Urns, bowls and Mutt

I'd like to take a closer look at the 'Ode on a Grecian Urn' and compare its treatment of the object with that of Wallace Stevens' 'Poems of Our Climate' – but with two provisos in mind. First, my writing about these poems, like any literary criticism, cannot snip the strings tying it to the objects addressed in the poems either. Having dwelled on the complexity of the relationship between a poem and its object, to the point of dismissing the separability of either from the other, it would be inconsistent to assume that the relationship between that poem and its criticism might be any easier (not that I plan to add to the remarks I made in the Introduction about different critical approaches). Secondly, I am writing about urns and bowls in a book on modern including modernist poetry, and the most notorious modernist bowl of all lies as far from the poetic as one can get – Duchamp's urinal of 1917, known poetically as 'Fountain'. The contrast between the elegant poems, both of which are both Romantic and neoclassical, and the pissoir that is functional in almost every sense (it's not plumbed in), could hardly be greater, and it points to a larger question – not about the use of poetry, but the use of objects by it. I wouldn't go so far as to say that a poem uses its chosen object to relieve itself upon it, but I would say that the idealization of objects that goes on in poems like those of Keats and Stevens goes together with the use-value of those objects in getting the idealization to occur – something that the cold porcelain of Duchamp cannily refuses.

I shall not parse every line, just comment on the famous first: 'Thou still unravished bride of quietness'.[7] The word 'Thou', though self-consciously archaic and disappointingly fusty for the otherwise erotic phrase, takes us straight into object-world. But the apostrophe doesn't just address the object; it posits it. The word 'Thou' is a calling or a beckoning as much as it is a detached address, and so it intervenes in the urn's otherwise unmolested state. And it does so to the point of picking it up as if on a forklift truck and depositing it in the poem itself; it posits the urn as much here as there, as much in the poem as in the imaginary space beyond it, such that the poem already becomes somewhat confused with its object; urn and poem embark on an isomorphic relationship. This is more than representation, for the urn in some sense depends on this intervention in order to gain phenomenological weight. The address calls the urn as addressable, as available to perception. Arguably, all poems begin with an invisible 'Thou', in the sense that before the words appear they were all on the point of addressing a subject, object, theme, event or person. This would render the word 'Thou' in the Keats poem an echo of a silent apostrophe that makes it possible.

The second word, 'still', could serve as a password to much of Keats' poetry: it braids together, for example, the inertia of 'Endymion' and the prolepsis of 'Isabella'. Its mystique stems from combining ideas of both time and space. Here Keats uses it mainly as an adverb, i.e. as a temporal term signifying 'as yet', and suggesting its having been translated out of Latin – the 'still-unravished-bride', somewhat like an ablative absolute. But it also alludes to the stillness of the urn as that urn occupies space. Because 'still' is also a noun – as in 'the still of the night' – there is even a hint of a set atmosphere surrounding the urn, a kind of private museum for study and speculation. In effect, the word 'still' encapsulates the central conceit of the poem, that of the figures on the vase being frozen in time, like the victims at Pompeii, trapped forever and paradoxically in a present participle. This is the 'now' that cannot divide itself in order to produce the next 'now' (also known as 'then'). Which in a sense defines the object. Although we all know that objects exist in time, and decay like everything else, they create the illusion of an indivisible now, and of their own inability to break themselves into temporal segments succeeding one another from left to right with time's arrow. The urn has to exist in the present for Keats to appraise it, but its stillness deceives, telling us that it exists in a much earlier time; the paralysed figures picked out upon it serve partly to give that illusion form and substance.

This false indivisibility of the now, as projected by objects, also offers a way of defining the form they take. A form, like that taken by an urn, is *formed*, and if it is formed, it means the object with that form pretends there was a moment in time at which it ceased becoming and switched over into being. Objects compel attention because as a presentation of form they seem to resist the temporal moment they find themselves in at any point. Or, if not 'attention', then a kind of existential jealousy of the kind evident in Keats' poem, especially as it is inflected in terms of a ravishment that cannot be consummated. I pity, but I also envy, your stillness, the poem seems to say to the urn, like I envy a death that can stay alive. In response, the urn, a kind of stone throat, has no response at all, for to respond is to place that trick of permanence in jeopardy, and so it has to listen, betrothed as it is to silence. Again the object becomes a sounding-box for the poet, a conch.

As I suggested earlier, this is all idealization, and idealization of the material to boot. The gratingly supercilious tone that Keats' poem sometimes adopts comes from a doctrinaire Hellenism married with an awful moralism culminating, having begun with one of English literature's best lines, 'Thou still unravished bride of quietness', with two of its worst: 'Beauty is truth, truth beauty', etc. The desire to exploit the object is all too apparent, and it reminds one of Nietzsche lamenting how bad philosophers are at seduction – poets could be even worse. Like the foster-child the unravished bride remains unassimilated.

Stevens' 'The Poems of our Climate' (which in the collected edition comes just before 'Prelude to Objects') goes through a similar temptation by objects only to reverse back towards the consolations of the questing mind that appraises them:[8]

I
Clear water in a brilliant bowl,
Pink and white carnations. The light
In the room more like a snowy air,
Reflecting snow. A newly-fallen snow
At the end of winter when afternoons return.
Pink and white carnations – one desires
So much more than that. The day itself
Is simplified: a bowl of white,
Cold, a cold porcelain, low and round,
With nothing more than the carnations there.

II
Say even that this complete simplicity
Stripped one of all one's torments, concealed
The evilly compounded, vital I
And made it fresh in a world of white,
A world of clear water, brilliant-edged,
Still one would want more, one would need more,
More than a world of white and snowy scents.

III
There would still remain the never-resting mind,
So that one would want to escape, come back
To what had been so long composed.
The imperfect is our paradise.
Note that, in this bitterness, delight,
Since the imperfect is so hot in us,
Lies in flawed words and stubborn sounds.

Here the object – a bowl of pink and white carnations – promises an idealization, and just about delivers it, only to then provoke dissatisfaction. The never-resting mind seeks imperfection to (dis)satisfy itself. The presence of those carnations carries an important qualification, however. The poet is not after the incarnation of the perfect, the ideal made flesh, but the imperfect that *is* our paradise, not a copy of it. The fact the poem assumes more or less the form of a syllogism – thesis, antithesis, synthesis – cleverly mocks scholastic attempts at reconciling heaven with earth.

On the other hand, the poem is hardly made up of 'flawed words and stubborn sounds' itself. It has the feeling of a 'perfect' or ideal poem, partly because of that tripartite form, partly because of the seaboard daylight, and partly because it and the bowl of carnations have a relationship with each other more subtle than that of a subject–object pairing. In a certain sense, the poem is the clear and brilliant bowl, not least because we, the reader, tend to confuse the object (the poem) with its subject (the bowl). The words of the poem are impure only in so far as they are not dissolved into the snowy air; and because they make that snowy air legible they achieve a beauty of their own. Moreover, being two-dimensional, those same words on the page remain merely virtual objects, free of the gross substance that even as delicate a thing as a bowl of carnations assumes. The poem is more like a mind than an object, and the objects it chooses to describe form part of its own intellectual substance.

The word 'cold' seems a deliberate reference to Keats' own 'cold pastoral'; both poems have about them the chill of the mausoleum, and both are propitiatory works too self-involved to be much use to the dead anyway. The never-resting spirit of the Stevens seems about to sweep the bowl off the table, impatient at poetry's obsession with things that are dead or still or perfect or pure. Perhaps there is even a swipe back at Keats too, and the insufferable romanticism of truth and beauty. The imperfect is so hot in us, and we are like a sizzling metal desperate for a mould, or a canvas for a frame, such is our daemon's rage for form. The object taunts our daemonic fluidity, our liquidity, with the temptation of permanence, and a whole genre of poems – the equivalent of still life in painting – has emerged in reaction. In modern poetry, this human drive to posit oneself with the endurance of a (beautiful) object can be understood as a displacement of an ancient, Homeric theme, to do with renown and reputation. At the start of this chapter I spoke about living on: the poetic object functions as this fantasy of eternal life, especially in terms of being thought of well. The fact that such objects are often hollow and literally capable of resonating therefore seems important. They can continue to drone the name of the poet.

There is an important somatic aspect too. The object in or of a poem has a body, be it an urn, a bowl, a coffin or a bee-box, and so too does the writing poet. The object gets measured against the poet's body, put into a scale. It is not so much that objects in poems are anthropomorphic, or that they represent their author in some subliminal way – though that may be true – it is rather that they remind us of physical being on the side of the poem, and so mirror the possibility of physical being on the side of the poet. Even the never-resting mind in Stevens has, in its evocation of insomnia, a bodily dimension, making of it a live, uncomfortable object that will have had a corresponding object in the body of Wallace Stevens. I am not saying that in writing the lines 'never-resting mind' Stevens was writing about his own body as it fidgets, just that there will have been a body of some sort attached to the writing implement that wrote the poem, and that when the poem furnishes itself with objects these have a relationship with that body. What is that relationship? It's not just psychological: it's the recognition that both take up space, real or virtual, on each side of the poem, and that between them there exists a 'strange attraction'.

Which in turn might involve something suggesting erotic control. The shell of the urn or bowl or box or coffin protects its precious interior while giving the perceiver or holder of it the sense of mastery, of comprehending it or enwrapping it – as if the perceiver were the casing of the casing, so to speak. It offers the opportunity of touch without responsibility. In Stevens the pink and white carnations, echoing the bride in Keats, suggest a nubile fleshliness encircled by the bone of porcelain, or bone china, forming an exoskeleton (think also of the exoskeleton of Plath's poem 'In Plaster',[9] and of the urn which has reversed the relation of the soft to the hard, the bodily ashes to the hard vessel). A delicate brittleness, an opening, the frills of the carnations, and the resonance of the male voice – it is a perfectly wrought sexual scene, set at an intellectual pitch.

One last remark. Because they are smaller, because their edges are more exposed, there is an empirical sense in which poems are more like objects than are novels. When a poem then treats of an object it is entering a particularly over-determined, perhaps narcissistic, space, in which objects become poems in another form – in a sense, Keats' urn is itself a poem, or is seen as a poem by the poem. Also a rarefied space: few novels will sustain interest in an object over several hundred pages, whereas to do so represents the poem's still life, a demonstration of its craft, an étude uniquely appropriate to the poetic instrument. If we want to understand the presence of an object through the medium of words, it is to the poem we will turn, and the poem rewards us with the joint finitude of both itself and the object it describes. All such objects are 'dead' in so far as they have been posed, styled, established to be looked at; they are not characters in a novel, whose motion is always possible. Poems are drawn to what doesn't change, and if there are such strong topoi in poetry to do with transience, with fading, with metamorphosis, they exist not for the poem to track that chromatic decline over time, but to portray the contrast in its hues – from crimson to indigo, say – on a single plane. It is this that allows the poem to observe things (objects) *in relief*, with a depth that might suggest movement without ever stirring, like Keats' urn. Gradients or textures of space that give the illusion of time, and create a layered object refracting the mind that perceives it: such is the poem that solicits its perfect object.

4

Hearing voices

What does it mean to have a poetic voice? How does 'voice' differ from style? What is its relationship to the 'music of poetry'? It is such questions that this chapter aims to address, but from within a wider hypothesis that, like a prayer which hopes to become enveloped and irradiated in the glow of the divine, poetic voice strives to transcend itself and become light – or, in less rhapsodic terms, to allow the word to be superseded by the image. In doing so the almost intolerable solipsism of the poetic finds relief in dispersal and clarification.

To get into this elusive topic, I start by quoting from (my preference would be to quote entirely) John Ashbery's 'Self-Portrait in a Convex Mirror' (1973).[1] The narrator has been musing on a painting by Parmigianino, as discussed by Vasari in his *Lives of the Artists*. Owing to the convexity, the painting shows 'the right hand' of the painter as 'Bigger than the head'. The painting's distinguishing feature prompts the narrator to wonder whether the soul of the subject can be captured: if a conventional self-portrait, painted with a flat mirror and (even when there is perspective) to look 'flat', is supposed to depict its subject's soul, does that soul have further to travel out of the picture when that picture turns into a sphere? Ashbery writes:

> The soul has to stay where it is,
> Even though restless, hearing raindrops at the pane,
> The sighing of autumn leaves thrashed by the wind,
> Longing to be free, outside, but it must stay

Posing in this place. It must move
As little as possible. This is what the portrait says.
But there is in that gaze a combination
Of tenderness, amusement and regret, so powerful
In its restraint that one cannot look for long.
The secret is too plain. The pity of it smarts,
Makes hot tears spurt: that the soul is not a soul,
Has no secret, is small, and it fits
Its hollow perfectly: its room, our moment of attention.
That is the tune but there are no words.
The words are only speculation
(From the Latin *speculum*, mirror):
They seek and cannot find the meaning in the music.

The lines, which in both the subject-matter and the pseudo-scholasticism of their investigations ultimately descend from metaphysical poetry, are freighted with the pathos of the atheist or scientist returning from a voyage of discovery only to report there was nothing to discover: 'the soul is not a soul'. If the soul cannot puncture the canvas, it is because its life is merely a reflection of the beholder's gaze, 'our moment of attention'. It 'fits/ Its hollow perfectly' because it is itself a kind of vacancy. Everything about the soul, lamentably, is 'speculation', mirrors and, by association, substanceless smoke. The tune has no words, the music no meaning; the convexity merely puffs out the emptiness that flat paintings disguise.

As for voice, one hears clearly that of Ashbery – the ambling disputatiousness, the mind behind it both sharp and dilatory, the defiantly prosaic and tenacious prosecution of a topic that, through the elegant obliquity of its observations, nevertheless achieves a 'poetic' effect over several lines. How does it do so? It has as much to do with the personality or 'sensibility' of the given poet as the given poem. What makes Ashbery important is that he helps invent what it means to be a modern poet after Eliot – still collegey, but no longer academic, with a brand much closer to that of the *New Yorker* than the *Criterion*. No militant modernist would have stooped to include the parenthesis '(From the Latin *speculum*, mirror)', as such knowledge on the part of the reader would have been assumed. Most of the disillusionment of the early twentieth century has been done by the time Ashbery arrives, most

of the angst expiated, which means it no longer oppresses, and
even the airy vacancy of the absent soul can provide a certain satisfaction. Ashbery's is the intellectual's weekending voice, cultured,
expansive, urbane, yet always dressed in comfortable clothes.

Does this 'voice' have a sound? After all voice is voice, that
which is vocal, enjoys sonority, breaks the silence; reading the
poem in our head shouldn't change that fact. But the sound made
by poetic voice is not quite the same as the sound made by words.
Take the lines

> The pity of it smarts,
> Makes hot tears spurt: that the soul is not a soul,
> Has no secret, is small, and it fits
> Its hollow perfectly

It is not hard to point out the sibilance and the plosives, nor how
well suited they are to the whispering closetedness of the soul they
depict. But the Ashbery voice is hardly explicable solely in terms of
these not particularly hard-won effects. Even if one were to parse
every last stroke of the verse, the voice would still escape, because
it functions mainly as a proxy for that personality of the poet as
inferred by the reader.

Voice cannot be reduced to personality, however: it is also made
up of cadence, the fall of a series of lines like the route taken by a
mountain stream as it zigzags downwards over stones. When, in
conjunction with the inferred personality of the poet, this idiosyncratic route gets duplicated over several poems, the reader can begin
to identify that poet's unique voice. Go back to the poem's opening:

> As Parmigianino did it, the right hand
> Bigger than the head, thrust at the viewer
> And swerving easily away, as though to protect
> What it advertises. A few leaded panes, old beams,
> Fur, pleated muslin, a coral ring run together
> In a movement supporting the face, which swims
> Toward and away like the hand
> Except that it is in repose. It is what is
> Sequestered.

and compare it with these lines from Ashbery's 'The Other Cindy':[2]

Sure, there was more to it
And the haunted houses in those valleys wanted to congratulate
You on your immobility. Too often the adventurous acolyte
Drops permanently from sight in this beautiful country.
There is much to be said in favor of the danger of warding off danger
But if you ever want to return
Though it seems improbable on the face of it
You must master the huge retards and have faith in the slow
Blossoming of haystacks, stairways, walls of convolvulus,
Until the moon can do no more. Exhausted,
You get out of bed.

The poems are different, but the voice is the same; and it is the
same not least because of the cadence, where cadence is the less
predictable cousin of metre, a semi-regular pattern of beats. The
Ashbery voice likes to unfurl ambitious sentences but just as
quickly furl them up, with such blank perorations as cap each of
the two quotes above – 'It is what is/ Sequestered', 'Exhausted,/ You
get out of bed'. In the course of this cadence we trace a movement
from active to passive, a movement with a view to becoming active
again. To add texture and colour, Ashbery stuffs its middle with
lists, as if to concretize what might grow too abstract: 'A few
leaded panes, old beams,/ Fur, pleated muslin, a coral ring' in the
first; and 'haystacks, stairways, walls of convolvulus' in the second.

Now, one could be more purist about it, and announce that
cadence trumps personality. One could argue that voice begins
where personality ends, that what carries it is the poem's cadence
rather than the poet's charisma. Besides, 'cadence' cannot fall
anywhere outside of language. Thus one could 'hear' an Ashbery
poem through a wall, say, and know it was an Ashbery. Under such
conditions, it wouldn't be personality that the listener would hear,
but a muffled music with a familiar set of aural contours. Together
such contours create 'voice' in the impersonal sense, the auditory
signature that recurs throughout a poet's oeuvre and remains with
the text.

Not that 'voice' translates as the 'music of poetry', at least in the
Eliotic interpretation of it whereby the music of a poem conveys
meaning both before and more profoundly than that poem's
words. According to this doctrine, any reader can get any poem
in any language, because the difficulties strewn by not knowing

another tongue can simply be stepped over. The music of poetry overcomes linguistic difference, as if it emanated from before Babel, operating as a universal. Voice, by contrast, adheres locally to a set of poems, even if it may be divorced from the poet who scribed them – or even if the poet's personality amounts to no more than an anthropomorphic effect produced by the cadence of a collection of poems grouped editorially and legally under the name of a single personage. True, the poetic voice can be 'musical' in the more restricted aesthetic sense that it comes with a tempo, a pitch, a tone, and so on, assuming that such terms are not just metaphors. But universal it will never be.

Or will it? Surely the axiom on voice in poetry is that it is distinctive. Hence my opening question as to whether between voice and style any difference obtains. Aren't the two terms interchangeable? I'd like to make a distinction, and argue that 'voice' is never pure, that it actually represents a tension between private and public ownership. It might not be universal, but nor is it entirely unique.

Poetic influenza

Consider Harold Bloom and his theory of an anxiety of influence.[3] Bloom claims that poets are influenced by earlier poets and spend their artistic careers in Oedipal battle to overcome that determinism and become individuated. Weak poets never quite overthrow their precursor, and are doomed to sound derivative. It is almost literally an influenza, a virus that cannot be shaken off, distorting the voice, blocking it up, infiltrating the poetic sinuses. Strong poets might sneeze but they never catch the cold, going on instead to become a health risk to future generations of poets.

Now, this Oedipal or paternalistic stress is arbitrary: the only theoretically durable element of Bloom's theory is the imitability of the voice, and there is nothing to say that such imitability must always be associated with the father. Bloom simply conflates the two things: first, the voice is imitable; second, poetic influence, which works by imitating a poetic voice against one's wishes, is paternalistic. I would like to isolate the first, and draw some different conclusions. For if the voice is imitable, it enjoys some independence, some detachability from whomever speaks with it. This independence of voice qualifies the originality of what in Bloomian terms would be the 'strong' poet – the Miltons, the Shakespeares, and so on. The imitability of the poetic voice implies that the poet who speaks with it doesn't entirely own it, or at least can't control its ownership. Even where that voice – say the Arnoldian voice, with its solemn moralism and restrained aesthetics – originates with a given poet, its imitability is already at work in the original, corrupting its purity. The voice exists in a virtual space between the poets who from time to time adopt it.

As well as this structural corruption, the originality of the original voice will in any case have been composed of heterogeneous elements. The voice of Matthew Arnold, for example, combines dulcet Hellenism, King James orotundity, edifying schoolmasterliness, and so on. The result might be original, but the ingredients are allsorts. Both strong and weak poets, in other words, speak with forked tongues, which means Bloom's ostensibly crude ordering into earlier and later poets is vital: what matters is who spoke first.

And there is a more disquieting aspect to this splitting of the voice. If one ranks the voice among the most intimate chambers of identity, then to allow one's voice to be confused with another's, with or against one's will, is to allow one's identity to become confused too. So who, really, is speaking in a poem? Or, so as not to confuse the poem's author with its narrator, the better question is: Who speaks the poem? I think this 'whoness' of the voice in poetry is crucial, and the alloyed quality of the poetic voice, based on both its structural imitability and its empirical mixture of components drawn from earlier poets, suggests it is always polyphonous. But it is not unlimited. The voice of Ashbery is different from that of Arnold, which means the polyphonies involved in each case are distinct. A poetic voice represents a limited polyphony, every chorus a solo.

Perhaps that is not so strange a proposition: even in the everyday sense 'voice' includes timbre, breath, pitch and mimicry, making it a multiple instrument to begin with. Equally, one could argue that the who that is voiced in a poem refers not only to the poet but also to the voice of others. This is because the voice in a poem needs to be heard, and so produces an affect on the part of its listener. It is the listener, in hearing the voice of the poem, who confers the who upon it. The 'who' has to be recognized as such, has to be heard, and this means the poetic voice travels on a wavelength with the voices of others, who in hearing it, in comprehending it, construe and 'speak' it. In any case, for a voice to be identified, for it to be identifiable, it has to produce more than one datum about itself. There must be at least two 'sounds' for its identity to be verifiable. Finally, it might be the case that the voice's splitting like a reed is what gives it its whoness, in the sense that its whoness dare not coincide with itself for fear of disappearing. In order to make sound, to exist in time, to spread itself over a series of lines, to produce variation in tone, to achieve the aural contours I mentioned earlier and so establish a profile, the voice needs to split away from itself. In philosophical terms, the identity of the voice depends on an internal difference; if it were 'pure' identity, it wouldn't be able to posit itself.

How does this multiple whoness of the poetic voice work in practice? Take this ditty by Yeats, called 'Memory':[4]

> One had a lovely face,
> And two or three had charm,
> But charm and face were in vain
> Because the mountain grass
> Cannot but keep the form
> Where the mountain hare has lain.

The poem both recalls and invents a folk proverb or playground chant, alluding among other things to 'One for sorrow, two for joy'. Making such allusions would not be viable if that to which is alluded were not capable of being alluded to, of being broken off from its context, and the same applies to 'Memory' itself. It can be quoted or imitated, such that the Yeats voice doesn't belong solely to Yeats. And because a folk proverb, the poem almost literally has other people speaking through it. It is poetry of the oral tradition, even if it complicates that tradition on switching in the third line from major to minor to make its enigmatic admonition about the mountain grass keeping the form of the mountain hare. At the same time, this oral quality, which carries a polyphony of its own, gets offset by the poem's stele-like feel of having been engraved on a stone, the living voices ossified into a gnomic commandment. Not that this completely arrests the play of polyphony: the commandment, like a law, exists to be invoked, revived by the voice of others.

I said voice in poetry represents a polyphony that is limited, however, and the limitation in 'Memory' finds an emblem within the poem itself, in the impression made on the grass by the hare. For all its multiplicity, poetic voice remains as singular as that undeniable pattern, that moment in time that cannot be reversed, that fact that face and charm are not able to redact. In this respect, Bloom is right: what matters about voice is that it exists in time, and that at a certain point in time it made an impression, such that when we hear it again it brings with it its own priority, like a memory of itself. The voice is 'historical'. I'm not just talking about recognition, about how we know a Yeats poem to be a Yeats poem, about the familiarity it produces. To have a poetic voice means to have already spoken, to have posited something as singular as the shape left by a hare on a mountain, in all its animistic mystery.

Obviously, that raises a chicken and egg question. How can a poet speak for the first time if his or her voice needs to have already spoken? In empirical terms, it does not make sense, but in both transcendental and affective terms, it might. Think of the experience of reading Shakespeare: phrase after phrase sounds like quotation, not because Shakespeare has been quoted so copiously since it was penned, nor because the poet might indeed be quoting from, say, Plutarch, but because each phrase appears perfectly to fill the slot intended for it. The right word lands at the right time, and this perfect fit creates the feeling on the part of the reader that the word was necessary and so echoed a pre-given order. Though nothing could be more contingent, inventive, creative or innovative than a Shakespearean paragraph, the 'voice' of Shakespeare makes each word sound as if it were the *mot juste*. The voice involves a quoting of itself, in this special sense of a saying of the previously understood right thing to say.

Style and the muse

All this talk of the multiplicity of the voice, however, asks to be set against what I take to be the more unequivocally singular features of 'style'. Yes, one can still speak interchangeably about, say, Akhmatova's voice and Akhmatova's style, but if there is a distinction to be made, it would be on the grounds that style denotes that which in a given body of work is irreducibly inimitable (which, just to be clear, is to take the author, as opposed say to genre, as the basic unit of style: it is the author whose style cannot be copied, whereas a genre such as prothalamium or satire can). But can it be the case? Is there anything in a poet's style that's not susceptible to imitation? Here is an utterly characteristic stanza by Geoffrey Hill, from 'LACHRIMAE ANTIQUAE NOVAE':[5]

Crucified Lord, so naked to the world,
you live unseen within that nakedness,
consigned by proxy to the judas-kiss
of our devotion, bowed beneath the gold

It is inconceivable that so strong a style could not be imitated, even parodied: the very strength of style is what builds its imitability. How much harder it is to copy the generic, or at least to copy the generic and have its original identified. So if such a thing as inimitable style does exist, we'd have to look beyond the imitable, and that means looking beyond the language. What cannot be recreated about this verse is that which is lost from it, that which is irretrievable even to the most cunning counterfeiter, namely the event of its composition and the conditions in place at the time. These might up to a point be reconstructed but never returned to, meaning they are lost, with the important proviso that the poem itself bears testament to its composition having taken place, and to the conditions that will have applied. The poem carries its event of composition irretrievably within it; it is branded invisibly with the circumstances of its birth. This, for me, would be the definition of 'style', that unrepeatably singular set of determinants that informed the poem, and which constitute its ineradicable, if finally undetectable, history. These determinants include not just the date(s) on which the verse was written, the cultural atmosphere and so on, but everything in the author's mind at the time. 'Style' is the imprint of the construction of the poem on the poem, always receding further into the past but maintained in the present by the poem that does and doesn't testify to it.

But my theme is voice, not style, and I have been arguing for its constrained plurality. There is, of course, a more conventional,

even classical, account of the multiplicitousness affecting the
poetic voice, to do with the muse and inspiration (as in Milton's
overture to *Paradise Lost*, 'Of man's first disobedience … Sing,
heavenly muse').[6] The muse speaks through the poet who channels
its vatic articulations. Because, or despite, the fact that this figure
of muse is 'classical', it works in divine ways. The poet's human
talents cannot help but be circumscribed, and his or her own voice
little more than a diverting warble. With sufficient application of
technique on the poet's part, however, that voice can be tuned like
an instrument for the god-like muse to deign to play. Typically the
instrument would be a harp across which the melodious winds of
divine mystery sweep, the harp a metaphor for voice box. The poet
thrills to its sublime glissando, while concentrating on capturing
those capricious winds as efficaciously as possible, like a sailor
adjusting a sail.

The caprice is an important aspect, the poet unsighted as to
when 'inspiration might strike'. Whether the deific muse will blow
its honeyed breath across the strings at all is a matter for anxiety.
It certainly cannot be relied on, so that the poet's voice remains in a
state of vigilance, a state that doesn't dampen the flame of surprise
and gift which signals the stirring of the muse's own purer sounds.
The poetic voice schools itself in silence – the danger being that in
speaking it will hear only itself in its trivial garrulity and thus be
deaf, when the time comes, to the other voice that calls it, calls to
call through it. From this perspective, the poetic voice represents
only a division within the wider category of divine intervention. If,
as I was saying in the last chapter, poets speak through objects like
urns, then poets get spoken through and used by gods as part of
their wider design.

Although the prospect of having one's poetic voice co-opted
by a godlike muse might at one level sound wondrous, there is an
ambiguity in being so 'used'. Possession by a god becomes hard to
tell apart from possession by a devil. Both beings are capable of
changing shapes and taking over the voice of humans. The most
vivid example would be automatic writing, such as Yeats himself
describes in *A Vision*,[7] in which the voice of imitability takes on
shamanic properties (properties not wholly absent from Bloom's
schema, for that matter), where the shaman occupies a crepuscular
zone between good and evil. This possessed voice might be capable
of giving enunciation to the most beauteous verse as it resonates

from the heavens, but it is equally prone to speaking diabolical rubbish. The devil who takes possession gets its subject to speak filth, shout imprecations and utter the foulest profanities.

Either way, good or evil, the idea that the poetic voice springs upstream from the mouth of the poet where it debouches carries a couple of implications. First, that it is intoxicatingly rich, almost too much for the human to take into the mouth; sacred or profane, there is an element of the nauseous in the extraneous music made by supernatural entities, and a corresponding reaction of momentary disgust. Secondly, to have the voice speak through the poet suggests sacrifice and the duty which destiny has meted out. The subjugation is a kind of calling or vocation, with the poetic voice expecting nothing in return. Its reward is paradoxically to give itself, making of itself a gift to the task that gives no empirical reward. It receives to the extent that it gives itself up, and as such is perpetually removed from any site where it might stand in expectation of returns. In being chosen, it gives itself away, forsaking identity and all claims to independent substance or subsistence. Perhaps this is why truly worldly poetry is so rare, its deepest instincts those that shrink towards innocence. After all, to be the mouthpiece of a muse is to surrender responsibility for one's utterances; the poet cannot be blamed.

No, the poet always defers to the muse, except that the muse remains behind a veil, guarding an innocence of her own. Poetry is this relay of blameless voices, and at its fount stands a goddess who speaks with wisdom and insight despite her purity. The fact the muse is conceived as female creates an interesting contrast, for sure, with Bloom's history of male struggle, but the main point is that poetic voice, according to this topos, is always secondary to its source of inspiration. The topos is arguably a Platonic construct, with the muse representing the ideal, the poet expressing its belated and feeble echo. In all cases, the muse per se cannot be adduced, and the resulting mystery lends to all poetic utterance an aura of the untouchable.

I said the muse was 'classical', so what became of it in modern poetry? It got replaced by a notion, verging on the popular, of inspiration; inspiration is a secular form of the random gift once dispensed by the muse. Yet the poetic voice remains as vulnerable to the whim of inspiration's appearances as it did to those of the muse. What's worse, being a poet now feels less like being a chosen seraph, and more like isolation. Inspiration might never strike, and the vigil is lonely. The modern poet is not in touch with the gods – even Geoffrey Hill's is a voice calling in the wilderness – and his or her inspiration is as likely to lurk in the sulphurous bog of the personal unconscious, with the 'voice' its air-vent, as in the trove of golden images that yields only temperamentally to the poet's attempts to raid it.

Whether it is towards a celestial muse or a local inspiration that the voice orients itself in order to charge its mouth with the content it will then express, they both represent an effacement of the poet's own voice, and a dazzling of it with almost unimaginably intense figures. The instinct to say something powerfully beautiful, the instinct by which the poetic voice is so governed, is suicidal or at least sacrificial. For the sake of that gift of beauty, it would give up everything about itself.

Poetry, if the word is sayable

To conclude, I turn to a poem by Yves Bonnefoy. I have chosen a poem in French to help recall the distinctions between voice and sound.[8] Remember that according to a doctrine of the music of poetry, this poem should be intelligible even to the reader who has no French, though I also provide an English translation beneath:

> Le mot ronce, dis-tu? Je me souviens
> De ces barques échouées dans la varech
> Que traînent les enfants les matins d'été
> Avec des cris de joie dans les flaques noires
>
> Car il en est, vois-tu, où demeure la trace
> D'un feu qui y brûla à l'avant du monde
> —Et sur le bois noirci, où le temps dépose
> Le sel qui semble un signe mais s'efface,
> Tu aimeras toi aussi l'eau qui brille.
>
> Du feu qui va en mer la flamme est brève,
> Mais quand ell s'éteint contre la vague,

Il y a des irisations dans la fumée.
Le mot ronce est semblable à ce bois qui sombre.

Et poésie, si ce mot est dicible,
N'est-ce pas de savoir, là où l'étoile
Parut conduire mais pour rien sinon la mort,

Aimer cette lumière encore? Aimer ouvrir
L'amande de l'absence dans la parole?

(The word *brambles*, you say? Then I think of
Those boats stranded in sea-weed
That children drag on summer mornings
With cries of joy through dark pools of water.

Because in some, you see, there are traces
Of a fire that burned there at the prow of the world.
– And on the blackened wood where time has left
The salt that seems a sign but vanishes,
You too shall love the shimmering water.

Brief is the flame that goes out to sea,
But when it is quenched against the wave,
The smoke is filled with iridescence.
– The word *brambles* is like this sinking wood.

And poetry, if we can use this word,
Is it not still, there where the star
Seemed to beckon, but only toward death,

Knowing how to love this light? To love
To open the kernel of absence in words?)

Bonnefoy's poem constitutes not only an intonation of his voice:
it is a poem about voice, about borrowing words and enunciating
them afresh in new contexts, about the word 'ronce' being taken
from the voice of another and put through the poet's own voice
box and turned against different contextual lights. This other
figure quoted functions partly as modern muse, partly as Socratic
interlocutor. And, as with the classical muse, this modern muse

lends the word '*ronce*' to this new saying by the poet in different
lights, but without the word ever quite being owned in turn by
both the voice speaking and, by implication, the poet. Perhaps the
wonderment at pronouncing the other's word is the wonderment
of not being able to exhaust the word in repeating it. Indeed this
poem belongs to a series that returns to the same word, as if it were
a fount.

Yet such inexhaustibility, while suggesting an aesthetic surplus,
appears to have been created by a different kind of persistence. It
might be less that the word can never finally be used up, and more
that, like the light later on in the poem, it continues to live despite
and after being burned up completely. It tarries even after its sense
has gone numb through repetition. Its power of signification is
burned away, like the vanishing of the sign in the '*bois noirci*' until
it signals only the power of vanishing, or the death which the poem
names in the penultimate verse. So often light has this quality for
Bonnefoy: the ambience of vanishing rather than the condition of
illumination.

If the word becomes light, it does so paradoxically in this
poem, through a kind of curfew, where it blackens itself out, and
where its circulation can no longer be supervised. The title of the
collection from which the poem comes is *Ce qui fut sans lumière*,
that which was without light, so the difference between darkness
and being without light, is the distinction with a difference that
Bonnefoy demands we accept if we are to take him in good faith.
The distinction recalls that of Plato's 'anamnesis', which means
'not forgetting' as opposed to 'remembering'. In Bonnefoy's case
the negative definition, or litotes ('that which was without'), has
all the power of anamnesis governing it, with the qualification
that no reserve of images, no form bank or image-repertoire ever
gets established, as it would in Plato. The transfiguring of word
into light takes place not with a view to an ideal word or an ideal
light – the word '*ronce*' is far too specific for that. Even if it can
be translated into English as 'brambles', the word '*ronce*' remains
untranslatable in this sense that its specificity belongs, in the French
language, to an irreducibly singular relationship between the poet,
the speaker of the poem and the '*tu*' to whom she or he responds.

I would also pick out the verb '*aimer*', to love. The first line of
the previous poem runs: '*Tu me dis que tu aimes le mot ronce*'.
The other loves this word, and sharing the fact itself becomes an

act of love. To tell someone what you love is perhaps incipiently to tell them that you love them, especially a word the intimacy of which can be reproduced in the other's voice (unlike the shared love for a painting, for instance). The vocalization of a loved word assists the growing responsiveness between those who share it, the spouses who respond and correspond: 'spouse' belongs to the same linguistic family as the word 'response', and even the word '*ronce*' is like a contraction of the French '*réponse*'. On this account, love is the capacity to suffer the voice of the other in one's own.

At the end of the poem come two uses of the verb:

Et poésie, si ce mot est dicible,
N'est-ce pas de savoir, là où l'étoile
Parut conduire mais pour rien sinon la mort,

Aimer cette lumière encore? Aimer ouvrir
L'amande de l'absence dans la parole?

Loving and knowing are brought together. Isn't poetry, if the word is sayable, knowing how to love, despite everything, the light of there where the star appears to lead, but for nothing if not death? Loving opening the almond of absence in the spoken word? Loving is then trying to bear the knowledge of a privation, which has a stoic valour to it. It means standing at the spot where the word runs out, where a recognition is voiced but not spoken – a distinction that I would still like to hold on to, a distinction perhaps akin to that between '*mot*' and '*parole*' in the poem. The poetic voice can be heard properly only through this loving-knowingness of it which is in turn poetry. The silent listening to silence discovers the almond of absence. (The word 'almond', incidentally, apart from referring to a particular house and landscape dear to Bonnefoy's heart, might also pick up on Celan's use of this image. The phrase '*l'amande de l'absence*' sounds very like Celan who also used the word, which in German is '*Mandel*', to refer back in turn to Osip Mandelstam.) There is an intrapoetic listening which instead of reaching closure applies a gentle pressure of opening. The poem as poetry tries to fall against this opening; it falls by attempting to voice itself. It is not self-reflexive, and by launching such open-ended questions the poem goes out of its way to suggest the most infinite distances preventing it from joining back on itself.

There is another complication in the qualification '*si le mot est dicible*'. Poetry, if this word is sayable. Poetry becomes the object within a poem of poetry's own concerns. Poetry, which voices the unspeakable or unsayable, finds itself naming itself as poetry, and then withdrawing from the identification finding that just as unspeakable too. The poem names poetry as if it (the poem) were a detached discourse whereas the naming takes place in nothing but the poem; when it tries to name poetry itself it is caught in a double loop. If 'voice' occurs here, it is as the appearance of its own crisis, as a cancelling out of the voice that can nevertheless be voiced in some minimal way. The poem tries to stage this crisis in terms of light, i.e. as the very condition of appearance. It is as if wrestling with the question as to what form poetic voice can take given that its powers of continuation are so oblique and rare. Poetic voice cannot help but be drawn to the idea that it might have appearance, and so falls in love with light. The art of poetry becomes that of knowing how to love the light with the knowledge of the light's fantastical vanishing.

All this implies that the poem's somewhat heroic landscape is less a means of dramatizing the pursuit of an elusive end at the risk of death, than the setting of its own emergence into a world of complete unlikelihood. This is the autobiographical rhythm of a voice that shares a word only to discover that the word is beyond sharing, its capacities for being responded to subsumed into a far more pressing dialogue passing only through the singular and the singular memory. But the memory is equally subject to breakdown, for it is a matter of traces and vanishings, recapitulations that carry little substance, and the poem mesmerizes itself with images of direction, dragging, traces, signals, promptings, departures, leading, etc.: the word '*l'absence*' in the final line means literally 'without direction or meaning'.

I am not claiming Bonnefoy's poem is definitive of 'voice' in poetry: it is too complex to be an exemplar. I am, however, saying that voice differs from style in that it is always plural to a limited degree. In the Bonnefoy poem, that plurality gets acted out explicitly with the citing of a word ('*ronce*') that never quite becomes a possession, creating a diffuse plangency not dissimilar to plainsong, an effect supported by the high incidence of abstract nouns and verbs.

Nor does Bonnefoy's topos of voice-becoming-light serve as a model for all modern poetry. Nevertheless it exposes a desire with more general application. Poetry loves voice as it loves time: both are media for what I earlier talked about as cadence, the flux of sound as it morphs within a range that allows it to be identified with a certain poet; and both allow for variation in tone. But that is all transient. Poetry also wants to make a deposit, to leave a trace that remains – nothing so gross as the real or the factual, but something with phenomenal quality, something that can be seen or, better still, something that allows things to be seen.

5

The flowers of rhetoric

I want in this chapter to examine the relationship between poetry and rhetoric. Because of the niceness of the one and the nastiness of the other, it might at first sight look like an odd comparison to make. But a reversal of these values can be imagined with little effort. Rhetoric might be a grave matter of persuasion, of oratory deployed in the course of public debate, but in order to be effective it will avail itself of those techniques and feints – digressions, embellishments, illustrations and metaphors – that make its arguments the more disarming. In doing so, it borrows vestments from the same dressing-up box that poetry uses to adorn itself. As for poetry, or modern poetry at least, recourse to pretty figures, whether in the service of influence or not, has been increasingly treated with suspicion. Part of the modernity in modern poetry lies in heavily moderating anything too flowery, with the result that it has developed a highly circumspect relationship to rhetoric considered as a repertory of linguistic devices.

Before enlarging on these themes, I'll add a couple of provisos, including the obvious one that to write a chapter 'on rhetoric' can be denounced as naive: it assumes that the language with which I talk about rhetoric can avoid being rhetorical. Nevertheless, let us recall the customary division of rhetoric into persuasion on the one hand, and the classification of oratorical devices on the other. When we think of rhetoric as persuasion it might be Plato's denunciations

of the Sophists that come to mind. According to Plato, the Sophists
ply you with mere rhetorical sophistry rather than speaking truth.
Their concern is to manipulate, not to elucidate, and in Plato's
eyes this practice represents a perversion of the noble function of
rhetoric, which is to provide a mechanism by which the human
mind can generate, in dialectical fashion, insights of an authenti-
cally philosophical nature. When, by contrast, we think of rhetoric
as classification we might recall Quintilian and Cicero, and the
fabulous names given to various rhetorical tropes – anacoluthon,
aposiopesis, prosopopoeia, and so on. Paul de Man summarizes:[1]

> on the one hand, in Plato for example and again at crucial
> moments in the history of philosophy [...], rhetoric becomes
> the ground for the furthest-reaching dialectical speculations
> conceivable to the mind; on the other hand, as it appears in
> textbooks that have undergone little change from Quintilian
> to the present, it is the humble and not-quite-respectable
> handmaiden of the fraudulent grammar used in oratory

Today it is the notion of rhetoric as persuasion that predominates.
Rhetoric is understood primarily in the sense of political
manipulation, and to this extent we 'moderns' are thoroughly
Platonic. At the same time, however, it is a feature of our modernity
that we believe everyone is entitled to their opinion, everything is
relative, and that absolute truths do not exist – these being the
conditions in which rhetoric thrives. This is where we depart from
Plato. We might be chary of 'rhetoric', on the grounds that it floats
free from the truth and becomes an exercise of spin; and yet we
are equally squeamish about affirming an absolute truth or set of
truths in the face of which rhetoric ought to bow down or out.
After all, rhetoric is the vehicle of interpretations and opinions,
which number among the primary means by which the modern
individual can express his or her independence of mind. Rhetoric
and interpretation unite in their shared relation to a final truth that
has been suspended.

And there is another reversal, for despite this popular suspicion
of absolute truth, poetry might still lay claim to it. This is because
poetry is one of the arts, and the arts are supposed to give access
to a realm not ordinarily visible, in which 'truth' might nevertheless
be glimpsed. It is OK for claims to truth to be made in the world

of aesthetics, partly because they scarcely impinge on real life but mostly because the truth at stake concerns such supposedly universal concepts as 'human nature'. What is more, such aesthetic truths are permitted to be 'rhetorical' in the sense that they can use all the accoutrements available to the artist. A poem is permitted to speak a general truth and with all sorts of ornament, whereas a person is permitted to speak only on his or her own behalf.

Rhetoric, political and poetical

With these positioning statements in mind, I turn to a poem by Dylan Thomas:[2]

> Especially when the October wind
> With frosty fingers punishes my hair,
> Caught by the crabbing sun I walk on fire
> And cast a shadow crab upon the land,
> By the sea's side, hearing the noise of birds,
> Hearing the raven cough in winter sticks,
> My busy heart who shudders as she talks
> Sheds the syllabic blood and drains her words.

That is the first of four stanzas, and it throws us straight into the arms of rhetoric. There are few phrases more overtly rhetorical than that with which the poem begins: 'Especially when'. It shoots onto the page with an orator's emphasis and urgency, as if we, the reader, were caught listening to a speech in a debating chamber, a speech now climbing the last few steps to its climax. It seizes us with a hand around the neck: it is an interpellation, and as such it demonstrates something fundamental to rhetoric. Namely, that for all its self-enclosing artifice, rhetoric concerns the *relationship* between speaker and listener – there's no rhetoric without affect. Rhetoric is designed to 'move' its audience, in not just the metaphorical but the literal sense of getting people to move from one side of the debating chamber to the other, their opinions having been swayed by the rhetorically adept speaker.

Which suggests a disconcerting want of stability on that audience's part: rhetoric can only work in the hairline crack running through the audience's sense of conviction; if the audience were intransigently convinced of a given position, there would be no moving to be done. The rhetoric of the orator goes together with the listener's capacity for self-doubt. This is the case even if part of what makes rhetoric rhetorical is actually the indifference of the rhetorician, as manifested by the rhetorical question. The 'engagement' demanded by rhetoric need only go one way.

For its part, the poem also strives towards a certain indifference, and the (rhetorical) relationship between poem and audience to some degree challenges our notion of what a poem should be. It is not just that a poem is entitled to clad itself *with* ornament – similes, rare adjectives, melodramatic ejaculations – but that it should *be* an ornament. As a kind of aesthetic medallion, a poem should demand little, if any, engagement from its reader/listener beyond aesthetic gratification. The reader of a poem ought not to be provoked, cajoled or hectored in the way that they might expect to be if transplanted to a political forum. The risk the poem runs in employing 'rhetoric' of this political kind is that it lends it too worldly an air, and so jeopardizes its status as 'poetic', as that discourse which sits on the edge of the world.

Sure enough, the next words redress this balance of rhetorical and poetic. The first line continues: 'Especially when the October wind'. Suddenly 'Especially when' sounds less like Demosthenes and more like Homer (the 'frosty fingers' in the next line perhaps carry a very faint echo of Homer's 'rosy-fingered dawn'). We are landed in a season – autumn, no less – that season of seasons for poetry, on account of its mixing the vital with the deathly. But 'Especially when' sounds so very close to 'as when', and we could still be dealing with an extended metaphor, deployed by the rhetor for effect, meaning that the play between the more rhetorical ('Especially when') and the more poetic ('the October wind') remains unresolved. The violence of 'punishes' in line 2 undoes the schoolroom alliteration of 'frosty fingers' and, what is more, creates a grotesque image in 'punishes my hair'. It sounds like an appeal for justice (rhetoric), told in horrible pictures (poetry), so now the balance of rhetoric to poetry reaches temporary equilibrium.

There must be moments at which the territory encroached on by poetry becomes out of bounds to rhetoric, and this is what happens in lines 3 and 4: 'Caught by the crabbing sun I walk on fire/ And cast a shadow crab upon the land'. It is still emphatic, it is still persuasive, but now any intent to move the audience has been crowded out by an introspective drama more like private confession. In fact, it goes further. If 'confession' suggests a fetid need to communicate, these lines get willingly trapped by their own words, forget the audience almost completely, and mutate into a private hymnal. Is this the origin of poetry as flowers? Is the 'rhetoric' of poetry that point at which devices no longer seek to make an interpellation, but get distracted by their own inner logic? And is that what distinguishes the flowers of poetry from the flowers of rhetoric? Though both poetry and rhetoric will deploy all sorts of linguistic techniques, it seems that poetry will use them to turn in upon itself, something the rhetor, despite the indifference involved in the rhetorical mode, can never risk if he or she is not to leave the audience entirely behind. Perhaps tellingly, the next stanza begins with the words: 'Shut, too, in a tower of words'.

If there is an interpellation made in the Thomas poem thus far, it lies less in the effect on the reader than within the poem, as it throws the speaking subject into kaleidoscopic disarray, walking on fire like an insect under the apocalyptic bloom of a mushroom cloud. The 'crabbing sun' becomes the figure of this riving of the subject's wholeness, the equivalent perhaps of the audience's self-doubt when listening to a master rhetorician. Here, the sun is that master. It picks up the speaker of the poem like a crab that can merely wiggle its legs in the air, ungrounded. It even foists a vocabulary on the speaker, insisting on the words 'crabbing' and 'crab' as if to drive a lesson home: the speaker is prevented from enunciating other words in the force of this repetitious insistence from the fiery sun. So the speaker (who is and isn't the same as the poet) is pressed inside the self, away from the public sphere of the rhetorical, only to find that self is as prone to division, uncertainty and manipulation as any audience in a debate. It is this 'hairline crack' within a poem that differentiates it from rhetoric, but which creates equal space for literary exercise; it is represented in the poem by the difference between the speaking subject and his shadow as created by that sun.

There are other, more conventional, devices in these opening lines: the antithesis of frost and fire, the anthropomorphosis of the coughing raven, and the repetition of 'hearing' (the latter an instance not only of pathos but of a complicated onomatopoeia whereby the word 'hearing' begins to sound like the noise of birds

that is its object). Such devices might be rhetorical in the sense
that they are ostensibly superfluous to the arc of meaning, but
their purpose could hardly be said to be to persuade the reader to
adopt a certain point of view. That said, the notion of rhetoric as
gratuitous embellishment belongs quite properly to poetry, except
that such embellishments don't simply add to a poem but constitute
its core. Poems might contain 'messages', but a poem that allows
message to dominate over ornament will be calling its status as
poem into doubt. It is a situation that incidentally illuminates a
complexity in the concept of rhetoric, which is both ornamental
in relation to any truth it seeks to express, and simultaneously
nothing but message: a complexity that poems should avoid. The
poet should be economical with his or her messages, privileging the
'how' of the poem's operation over the 'what'.

What about the extraordinary last two lines of the stanza?:

My busy heart who shudders as she talks
Sheds the syllabic blood and drains her words.

The speaker appears to be overwhelmed by the voice of 'she', which
exacerbates the pre-existing condition of the speaker's 'busy heart'. It is
in an effort to withstand its rhetorical power, it seems, that the speaker
strives to shed the syllabic blood and, like a medieval doctor, drain
her words. After the cacophony of the birds, after the molestations of
the sun, this voice that makes him shudder is too much. The blood
needs to be drained as if reducing the pressure of rhetoric to silence,
to screen it out in the name of an albeit stymied private monologue.
This could be taken as an allegory of the relationship between poetry
and rhetoric, the former trying to turn the volume down on the latter
and slip out from under its temptations.

The second verse opens with a gloomy corrective:

Shut, too, in a tower of words, I mark
On the horizon walking like the trees
The wordy shapes of women, and the rows
Of the star-gestured children in the park.
Some let me make you of the vowelled beeches,
Some of the oaken voices, from the roots
Of many a thorny shire tell you notes,
Some let me make you of the water's speeches.

The speaker now turns to examine the tools of his trade, the words with which he works and which, through a process similar to synaesthesia, articulate the shapes of women who are already fashioned out of words. The confusion of word with thing carries through to the trees, the 'vowelled beeches' and 'oaken voices' that literally speak for themselves, lending the poet the implements with which to sketch them while withdrawing into their own self-sufficiency. It is a vision of flesh made word, and its consequence is to place any kind of rhetorical mastery on the poet's part at a decisive remove. The best he can hope for is that some will 'let him' craft images adequate to the 'you' he yearns to describe. Again we, the reader, get an account of the poet in a state of loss, of struggling in vain to make ground on his own voice, thanks to the masterful self-possession that precedes him in the shape of women, children, trees and so on. As if rhetorically complete, they have already realized themselves as words and 'speeches', leaving the poet to catch up pitifully with a fait accompli. Which positions poetry as the attempt to close the gap on itself, and poems as what flowers in that gap.

The poem's second half continues as follows:

Behind a pot of ferns the wagging clock
Tells me the hour's word, the neural meaning
Flies on the shafted disk, declaims the morning
And tells the windy weather in the cock.
Some let me make you of the meadow's signs;
The signal grass that tells me all I know
Breaks with the wormy winter through the eye.
Some let me tell you of the raven's sins.

Especially when the October wind
(Some let me make you of autumnal spells,
The spider-tongued, and the loud hill of Wales)
With fists of turnips punishes the land,
Some let me make you of the heartless words.
The heart is drained that, spelling in the scurry
Of chemic blood, warned of the coming fury.
By the sea's side hear the dark-vowelled birds.

There are some stand-out phrases: 'wagging clock', which again has a synaesthetic effect or at least makes a false ascription, the wagging relating not to a hand on the clock, which in any case should be a finger, but to the clock itself; 'the neural meaning', which sounds so clinically modern it wouldn't be out of place in Prynne; the Shakespearean 'wormy winter'. But I am aiming not to produce a lit crit on this poem so much as draw out questions of poetry and rhetoric, and what these last two verses share in particular with 'rhetoric' is their dependency on repetition, perhaps rhetoric's super-trope. The table below shows the extent of such repetitions in the poem:

Repetitions in Dylan Thomas' 'Especially when the October wind'

Later phrase	Earlier phrase
wagging clock	frosty fingers
hour's word	drains her words
windy weather	October wind
in the cock	the noise of birds
some let me make you	some let me make you
tells me all I know	tell you notes
the raven's sins	hearing the raven cough
especially when the October wind	especially when the October wind
wormy winter	winter sticks
fists of turnips	frosty fingers
punishes the land	punishes my hair
heartless words	my busy heart
my heart is drained	drains her words
chemic blood	syllabic blood
dark-vowelled birds	vowelled beeches

Some of the repetitions are exact, some half-exact, and some closer to association than repetition; but the overall effect cannot be denied. What is that effect? Not quite that of incantation or fugue, though it stimulates in the reader's mind a comparable inebriety: it is a sense of magic and mirrors, of a twisted but unavoidable logic, of an equation that, despite the colourful algebra of its terms, balances out. How does it differ from the use of repetition in classic rhetoric – (the famous example being the speech by Martin Luther King in which he uses the phrase 'I have a dream' eight times in succession)? Again, there is a point about message. The inescapable anaphora in the King speech is designed to cascade relentlessly into every ear until it is full, until the vision it portrays has been painted on the inner screen of all who listen; that is repetition as evangelism. Poetry must be wary of it on those grounds. Where possible, poets should, like Thomas, insinuate into the repetitions some subtle variation, unless the function of those repetitions is solely to mark out a formal pattern, like gridlines for a new building. The reason being not only the avoidance of message in the narrowly political sense, but the properly poetic opportunity to photograph the delicacies of shade that exist where repetitions are not quite exact.

But there is a more important value that repetition bears for the poet, to do with the establishing of a lexicon. Again, poetic differs from political rhetoric in this respect. The latter has to be careful to keep to an idiom that is broadly demotic, to ensure popularity. Poetic rhetoric, by contrast, embraces repetition and variation within repetition in order to limit, rather than expand, the list of words on which it might draw, in the name of constructing an image-world answerable only to its own logic. It aims to create a 'pull' towards it, rather than the 'push' given by political rhetoric. So when Thomas writes 'With fists of turnips punishes the land', it obviously chimes with 'With frosty fingers punishes my hair', and in such a way that we accept the second line as consistent with the poem's molecular structure, so to speak, even if the idiom in both cases is strange to the point of being repellent. The first phrase breaks open a path for the second, helping to construct the poet's own territory, a territory that we, the reader, now tend to accept on its own terms. Contrast it with these lines, say, from 'Chomei at Toyama' by Basil Bunting:[3]

Hankering, vexation and apathy,
that's the run of the world.
Hankering, vexation and apathy,
keeping a carriage wont cure it.

Keeping a man in livery
wont cure it. Keeping a private fortress
wont cure it. These things satisfy no craving.
Hankering, vexation and apathy ...

Plenty of repetition there, and the danger is that it throws over
poetic diction altogether, becoming indistinguishable from the
grousing of an old man in public. It is the rhetoric of a bore: just
as well Bunting uses it self-consciously to put the poeticism of the
poem in question.

Thomas won't take as many risks. His repetitions not only
steer clear of the political, despite the opening 'Especially when';
they help to license other experimental moments in the poem. For
example:

The heart is drained that, spelling in the scurry
Of chemic blood, warned of the coming fury.

It is not easy for the reader to nail down a meaning for 'spelling
in the scurry/ Of chemic blood'. Does 'scurry' denote the mess
of an ink made of blood? Is the heart therefore a blood inkwell?
Or is it the pen that spells? If so, is 'spells' supposed to remind
us of 'spills'? Is there even a connection between 'spelling' as in
orthography, and 'spells' as in magic formulae that might, among
other things, warn of a coming fury? The phrase is mysterious
and not completely yielding, yet within the lexicon of the poem, it
makes a certain sense. To be precise, it makes a peripheral, intuitive
rather than cognitive sense, and one hears or reads it in the way
one reads a foreign text while learning the language. It enjoys a
consanguinity with the phrases around it, from which the reader
or listener infers its general meaning.

Perhaps, in the case of this lexicon-building by the poet, the
trope of 'repetition' gets overtaken by a figure more like a spiral
or orrery, with the repetitions not quite coinciding but nevertheless
orbiting one another within a defined and predictable solar system.

There is, as it were, a gravitational pull that every part of the poem exerts on every other part, creating a tension. Which is not to argue for the unity of a given poem, so much as the unity of that lexicon, which will be dispersed across a whole group of poems. The repetition of a word or figure can achieve extra rhetorical force in an individual poem, if the same word or figure appears elsewhere in an oeuvre. Why is it rhetorical, exactly? Because the repetition helps to build its acceptability, and therefore to whittle away at the reader's resistance to it – which is another definition of persuasion. We, the reader, are 'persuaded' of a poet's work when it deploys an identifiable idiom, identifiable precisely because of its repeated elements.

Classification

Although I have been working with a distinction between poetic and political rhetoric, I have kept generally to the broad notion of rhetoric as the living practice of persuasion – the time-honoured convergence of logos, pathos and ethos – as opposed to the dead register of tropes. So the outstanding question is to what degree poetry might be 'rhetorical' in this more academic sense. How far is poetry merely an encyclopedia of literary devices?

Think first not of modern poetry, but modern art: movements such as De Stijl, cubism, Vorticism, constructivism, Bauhaus, and artists such as Mondrian, Picasso, Popova, even Nicholson. To a degree, the modernity of these 'modernists' lies in their making the workings of their works explicit. Rather than decorously burying technique in favour of a surface rich in content, they put forth an almost industrial account of the work's design. (Behind it, though with varying proximity, stands a broadly Marxist doctrine of demystification, the idea that artworks should dispel the bourgeois illusion that their conditions of production were not material, historical and economic.) And although this stance towards the artwork might indeed be 'modernist', it is nothing short of rhetorical, in the sense of foregrounding the elements of technique. A Mondrian can be experienced as much as a 'study' as a 'work', a study that details the 'rhetoric' of painting as consisting of, say, the relationship of contiguous blocks of colour, the geometry of line, the composition of shapes, or the interaction between figure and ground.

What, if any, equivalents to such artists exist in modern poetry? And does the 'rhetoric' of poetry, defined as the more or less explicit classification within a poem of poetic tropes, appear only among modernists? In answer to the second question, one might think back to the artificiality of Augustan poetry, for example, which delights in showing off its dexterity with Latinate devices and syntax. It might not *classify* every trope per se, but it will make its virtuosity pealingly clear to its reader, who is thereby invited to note each use of a phrase that could have come from Horace, Juvenal or other paragons of the rhetorical art. So no, the notion of a 'rhetoric' of poetry might not be exclusively modern and/or modernist; but the form it takes in Mallarmé, for example, suggests an innovation, which I'll try to describe.

At first blush, the experimentalism of Mallarmé, its far-fetched inventions and surrealist conceits, will seem a far cry from the dry domain of rhetoric. If anything, there is a bending of all rules of language, most apparent in 'Un Coup de Dés N'Abolira Jamais Le Hasard', with its flinging of words across the page as if out of a paint pot.[4] Yet Mallarmé remains a remarkably 'formal' poet, often ascetic in his adherence to the strictures of poetic discipline. The very figure of the poet is, in his eyes, one who has subdued the divine gift of imagination to the exigencies of what I would call rhetoric. At the same time, what the poet's imagination witnesses has to be revealed or it is no poetry at all. Hence in Mallarmé a distinctive tension between the restrained and the exorbitant.

I shall focus in on Mallarmé's homage to his beloved Théophile Gautier, 'Toast Funèbre',[5] a title that instantly suggests and calls for a rhetorical orderliness that will be sustained by the choice of solemn, politic alexandrines. The notion of a toast also connects back to Mallarmé's poem 'Salut',[6] a word denoting not just 'salutation' but 'health', and which also serves as the first word of the next line of 'Toast Funèbre'. All in all, there is a sane propriety to be maintained and both poems instantly position themselves as respectful of a pre-set order of language; the toast or salutation doubles as a recognition of poetic decorum per se and the rhetorical observation it imposes.

'Toast Funèbre' immediately makes that toast real in its inaugurating apostrophe: '*O de notre bonheur, toi, le fatal emblème!*' ('O fatal emblem, thou, of all our happiness'). The fact the apostrophe, on account of inverting the normal word order, takes the form of anastrophe gives an equally immediate self-consciousness to the poem, a self-consciousness enhanced by the fact that 'O *de*' can be heard as 'Ode', the salutatory toast an ode. We have barely breached the poem's interior, and we are being held under the lintel of its entrance arch, so to speak, made to appreciate the almost sacerdotal role the poet is taking on as he prepares his eulogy so fastidiously – even if, at the same time, that pun on 'O *de*' releases into the atmosphere a strangely delinquent note.

We find a similar mixture of the decorous and the subversive at the poem's other end:

> C'est de nos vrais bosquets déjà tout le séjour,
> Où le poëte pur a pour geste humble et large
> De l'interdire au rêve, ennemi de sa charge:
> Afin que le matin de son repos altier,
> Quand la mort ancienne est comme pour Gautier
> De n'ouvrir pas les yeux sacrés et de se taire,
> Surgisse, de l'allée ornement tributaire,
> Le sepulcre solide où gît tout ce qui nuit,
> Et l'avare silence et la massive nuit.

> (We dwell in those true groves, where, having marked our way,
> With large and humble gesture the pure poet must
> Stand guard against the dream as enemy to his trust:
> So that upon the morning of his high repose,
> When the task of ancient death for Gautier is to close
> His sacred eyes and keep his secrets, shall appear,
> As tributary ornament of the corridor,
> The solid sepulchre where all things harmful lie,
> And avaricious silence and night's immensity.)[7]

The epistrophe of '*nuit*' and '*nuit*' turns out in fact to be a case of paronomasia (rather like '*pur a pour*'), and what was in any case a bizarre rhyme – bizarre because too perfect – becomes more bizarre still. A formal ending has been achieved but at the expense of satisfaction, unravelling the close-knittedness it had at one level brought off; the couplet could come from a rhetorician's textbook aiming to demonstrate paronomasia regardless of the ugliness of the effect. One is left with a disconcerting cognizance of the poem's artificiality, despite the graveness of the context. How to square these opposing tendencies?

There is a fundamental sense in which all language is rhetorical, and that to construct a poem out of language means putting together a modular, flat-pack structure comprising different rhetorical components. In this sense, every poem can be stripped down to its parts, and proved to be 'rhetorical' through and through. The next question is how far a poem, in reassembling itself, will hide or reveal those component parts. Mallarmé seems to want to have his cake and eat it, such that this poem points not just forward to a brash modernity comfortable with disclosing the secrets of its assemblage, but back to an almost theosophical romanticism, in which rhetorical devices are to be tolerated solely as 'correct form' in the social sense.

But he also goes further, and there are clues in the content of that last stanza – admittedly ambiguous clues, given the cryptic quality (the 'amphibologia', to use the rhetorical term) of the lines. Mallarmé, or the speaker of the poem, seems to be defining the role of the 'pure poet'. First, they must be humble, and shun the tempting 'dream' that threatens to take them away from their duty, choosing instead an impassive silence that resembles the corpse of Gautier with its closed eyes and mouth, and that will facilitate the 'morning of his high repose'. In this self-denying regimen lies the possibility of a troika of the sacred, the deathly and the transcendental. Perhaps that suggests a not uncommon linking of poetic to religious aspirations, but what is interesting is that this conjuncture gets played out in so rhetorically rich a fashion. It is as if such soaring states of being can be accessed only through rhetorical profusion, as manifested in the paratactic puzzle of the single sentence that makes up the stanza just quoted – for example, the absence of an expected '*que*' to follow the opening proposition, '*C'est de nos vrais bosquets*', and the oddly supernumerary last line with its '*Et … et*' construction (a construction that is used quite ordinarily in French to mean 'both … and', but which in the context operates like a polysyndeton, an excess of conjunctions). At once under and over-charged with rhetorical devices, this climactic, admonitory sentence suggests that such devices do not just furnish the building blocks of poetry, but the moral characteristics of the poet.

On this account, 'rhetoric' becomes interchangeable with virtue, not just as the attempt to rein in those clamouring, siren-like dreams in the name of emotional discipline, but as that basket of poetic competences that may be exhibited to those who may judge. This is a long way from the schoolbook notion of rhetoric as academic correctness. Rhetoric and the poetry manufactured from it might be reducible to a set of tropes, but the poet who employs them does so as if they were individual muscles flexed in an ascent towards not just aesthetic but religious perfection.

Les fleurs

I have used the term 'the flowers of rhetoric', and by way of conclusion, I will make a brief comment on it. It is those afore-mentioned tropes such as epistrophe and paronomasia that count as rhetoric's 'flowers', its grace notes; though I repeat the point that these 'grace' or 'gratuitous' elements actually form the core. Other basic points include the following:

1   Being a metaphor, the phrase 'flowers of rhetoric' is itself rhetorical.

2   If rhetoric is made up of 'flowers', it is because flowers are seen as pleasing adornments, which supports the (highly contentious/easily dismissed) point that rhetoric is additional to 'normal' language.

3   If rhetoric is made up of 'flowers', rhetoric is literary, even though, as an instrument of persuasion, it might get used more often in a public and/or political environment.

4   If a flower is the ultimate literary object – the equivalent of a nude in painting – and rhetoric is made up of metaphorical flowers, it is a kind of metaphorical literature.

5   Choosing flowers as a subject in a literary text counts as 'flowery' regardless of the floweriness of the rhetoric; doing so confirms the literary text's literary credentials even if that text assumes an anti-literary manner.

6   Though flowers can be either male or female, the
    floweriness of the flowers of rhetoric has associations with
    the feminine, as does poetry itself.

7   While flowers are mostly seen as pleasing adornments,
    when they are treated of in poetry they frequently take on
    unpleasurable aspects – the most striking example being
    Baudelaire's '*fleurs du mal*' – and thus qualify the otherwise
    irenic notion of the 'flowers of rhetoric'.

In order to make some less telegraphic last remarks, I turn to
'Bavarian Gentians' by D. H. Lawrence:[8]

Not every man has gentians in his house
in soft September, at slow, sad Michaelmas.

Bavarian gentians, big and dark, only dark
darkening the daytime, torch-like, with the smoking blueness of
Pluto's gloom,
ribbed and torch-like, with their blaze of darkness spread blue
down flattening into points, flattened under the sweep of white day
torch-flower of the blue-smoking darkness, Pluto's dark-blue daze,
black lamps from the halls of Dis, burning dark blue,
giving off darkness, blue darkness, as Demeter's pale lamps give
offlight,
lead me then, lead the way.

Reach me a gentian, give me a torch!
let me guide myself with the blue, forked torch of this flower
down the darker and darker stairs, where blue is darkened on
blueness
even where Persephone goes, just now, from the frosted September
to the sightless realm where darkness is awake upon the dark
and Persephone herself is but a voice
or a darkness invisible enfolded in the deeper dark
of the arms Plutonic, and pierced with the passion of dense gloom,
among the splendour of torches of darkness, shedding darkness
on the lost bride and her groom.

As if to concentrate the intrinsic literariness of the generic flower,
Lawrence brings in the mythological depth associated with gentians

in particular, the flowers used to light the passage between the worlds of the quick and the dead. Again the main trope is that of repetition – 'dark' and 'darkness', 'blue' and 'blueness', 'torch' and 'torch-like' recited over and over. The second term in those repetitions, 'darkness', 'blueness', and 'torch-like' are technically cases of proparalepsis, the adding of a syllable to the stem word, making that word appear to unfold its petals. This is one of two ways in which this poem 'becomes' the flower it describes, in a hyper-rhetorical fashion. The other way is through the repetitions producing an almost painterly thickness, like an impasto: the result being a literary image that begins to 'look like' the indigo of the gentian. In the Chapter 4, I wrote about voice becoming light, and this Lawrence poem inches along the same axis, the words becoming saturated, through repetition, with the dark blue that nevertheless throws out a certain light – an effect reinforced by the image of the flower, with its five-pointed star, that we, the reader, might carry in the mind.

There is also 'repetition' in the lexicon-building mode evident in the Dylan Thomas. Like a baker kneading dough, Lawrence produces different shapes from the same material. Thus 'darkness spread blue' becomes 'darkened on blueness', as if he had folded the tacky poetic substance inside out or over upon itself. It is a species of homoousias, every part of the poem instinct with every other part, and it has rhetorical force again through gradually but inexorably cultivating the reader's familiarity with a lexicon that, despite the Miltonisms ('sightless realm', 'darkness invisible', 'arms Plutonic', and the wider echo of Satan's precipitous fall), starts out as alien. That reader is put in the position of learning the language of the poem, being inculcated in it, and so having his or her immunity weakened – exactly the result that rhetoric, as the medium of persuasion, aims at. From this perspective, the flower of rhetoric that is the gentian becomes the ensign of a foreign juris-diction, symbolizing an unfamiliar set of codes that nevertheless boasts its own sovereign logic. In the way that every poem stands sovereign in the poetic land it inhabits, accountable to nothing other than its own modus operandi, this flower of rhetoric taps its energy from a defiant isolation.

PART TWO

Readings

6

Darkling

I would like to offer a meditation upon the word 'darkling', especially as it appears in four poems: Keats' 'Ode to a Nightingale', Tennyson's *In Memoriam*, Matthew Arnold's 'Dover Beach' and Thomas Hardy's 'The Darkling Thrush'.

These four are by no means the only appearances made by 'darkling', though it is notable that they are possibly the four most famous poems of the nineteenth century, as if the word were a hallmark. Others from the nineteenth century abound. They include that by Byron in 'Darkness' (1816):[1]

I had a dream, which was not all a dream.
The bright sun was extinguish'd, and the stars
Did wander darkling in the eternal space,

Mary Shelley had it in her lyric of 1839, 'Oh, come to me in my dreams, my love!':

But gentle sleep shall veil my sight,
    And Psyche's lamp shall darkling be,

Robert Browning in 'A Grammarian's Funeral', written in the 1850s, goes:

Sleep, crop and herd! sleep, darkling thorpe and croft,
    Safe from the weather!

Elizabeth Barrett Browning, in 'Past and Future', has:

> Yet I find some good
> In earth's green herbs, and streams that bubble up
> Clear from the darkling ground

Rudyard Kipling's 'The Bell Buoy' of 1896 features it here:

>   He wars with darkling Powers
> (I war with, a darkling sea)

And so on.

Not that the popularity of the word 'darkling' started in 1800 and ended in 1900. There is a smattering of twentieth-century usages, as in the title 'Darkling Summer, Ominous Dusk, Rumorous Rain' by Delmore Schwartz. Lynne Crosbie has it in 'The Fly' ('darkling, drop of ink'); and Jennifer Scappettone has it in '... (In Exion)' ('darkling you weren't'). Prior to the nineteenth century, Charlotte Smith put it in 'Huge Vapours Brood Above the Clifted Shore' of 1798:

>   [...] the ship-lights faintly shine
> Like wandering fairy fires, that oft on land
> Mislead the pilgrim; such the dubious ray
> That wavering reason lends, in life's long darkling way.

Yet that 1798 date belongs to the same nineteenth-century trajectory that includes Keats et al. It is certainly hard to imagine the word cropping up much in the neoclassical era preceding it, though despite its absence in Chaucer's original, it enjoys a surprising cameo in Dryden's 1700 translation of *The Wife of Bath's Tale*:

> And where the jolly troop had led the round,
> The grass unbidden rose, and mark'd the ground:
> Nor darkling did they dance, the silver light
> Of Phoebe served to guide their steps aright,

According to the *Oxford English Dictionary*, the word 'darkling' can be traced back to 1450, half a century in any case after Chaucer. It appears in both Shakespeare and Milton, and its presence in the works of these two masters provides one of the reasons why it established itself so forcefully in the nineteenth century: if only because these titans of literature had used it, 'darkling' had the stamp of the literary.

But are there other reasons why it enjoyed such a nineteenth-century uptake? I think that, in so far as such periodizations are valid, part of the answer lies in the nature of the transition from the Romantics to the Victorians, a transition marked by a new sense of what I'd call 'poeticism'. From Charlotte Smith onwards for at least a century, poets develop an ear not just for what counts as literary, but as poetic. What is the distinction?

Literariness, on my definition, is what the typically neoclassical poet achieves when he or she elects the appropriate word or phrase for the context, what is 'appropriate' being that which obeys the precepts of a tradition. A form of orthodoxy, literariness looks back to previous literature, especially classical – Dryden's own relationship with Horace being a good example. It is conservative, tasteful and proper. If 'darkling' turns up less frequently in the century or so preceding the nineteenth, it is because its conservative, tasteful and proper qualities fall short. No doubt this is due to the word's origins lying not in Latin or Greek but what are perceived to be the relatively uncouth Germanic languages; it has in its past a pagan roughness, an unshaven folkness, which was perhaps the otherwise proper Dryden's justification for using it in his translation of Chaucer.

Poeticism, by contrast, cares less for literary precedent. Although poets will use 'darkling' because it has entered the poetic lingua franca, it is not the validation from having been used by other poets that is primarily sought. Rather, it is the affect, the mood, the climate, the dramaturgy of the poem then and there that matters; and 'darkling', draped in gothic velvet, uncanny and mysterious, suits the requirement of poeticism very aptly. It is conceivably the most 'poetic' word in the English language. More visceral than cerebral, to be poetic means to wring intensity from language that can immediately be felt. That said, poeticism is not an animal but an aesthetic quality. It is felt in the mind – felt in the mind as opposed to 'thought in the mind' or 'felt in the body', even if in this case the word 'darkling' makes the hairs stand up on the back of the neck. And because unfettered by precedents, poeticism looks instead toward innovation and originality, startling conjunctions, unforeseen juxtapositions, bold combinations.

So the rise of 'darkling' in the nineteenth century coincides with a rise in poeticism, in inverse proportion to literariness. It is a symptom of modernity construed as the relief from having to observe (neo)classical precedent, and it speaks to a new freedom of expression whereby the poet may draw as much on inner, psychological and affective resources as the outer, officially sanctioned staples of the literary canon. Tracking it across that century is like mapping the secret transmigration of a small, dark bird.

Keats (1819)

I cannot see what flowers are at my feet,
    Nor what soft incense hangs upon the boughs,
But, in embalmèd darkness, guess each sweet
    Wherewith the seasonable month endows
The grass, the thicket, and the fruit-tree wild;
    White hawthorn, and the pastoral eglantine;
        Fast-fading violets cover'd up in leaves;
            And mid-May's eldest child,
    The coming musk-rose, full of dewy wine,
        The murmurous haunt of flies on summer eves.

Darkling I listen; and, for many a time
    I have been half in love with easeful Death,
Call'd him soft names in many a musèd rhyme,
    To take into the air my quiet breath;
Now more than ever seems it rich to die,
    To cease upon the midnight with no pain,
        While thou art pouring forth thy soul abroad
            In such an ecstasy!
    Still wouldst thou sing, and I have ears in vain—
        To thy high requiem become a sod.[2]

Given its length and fame, I have not quoted the ode in its entirety, but supplied enough, I hope, to show how 'Darkling' fits in. In the sheer fact that the word is followed by the first person pronoun, we can observe the shift from the objective world of the literary to the subjective world of the poetic. To write 'Darkling I listen' is immediately to ascribe it to a personal state, to attach it to a sensibility that can now acquit itself as poetic on account of that attachment.

This subjective, poetic state characterized by Keats as 'darkling' involves an intricate confusion of sight, sound and smell. The speaker cannot see the flowers, though the word 'sweet' suggests he can smell them. On the other hand, the lines say he cannot 'see' their 'soft incense', as if that had at some point been a possibility. Unless it is a grammatical error forced by the metre and/or the rhyme scheme – after all, 'guess each sweet' is pretty clumsy – 'see' is either a metaphor for 'smell' (unlikely), or there was a way in which he might have expected to 'see the incense'. Is he thinking of the clouds of incense in a church, and projecting onto the flowers the image of their own 'incense', an incense that is in any case only metaphorical and releases only invisible clouds?

We might want to answer that with a relatively uncomplicated logic: the speaker cannot see, and he may or may not be able to smell, but he can listen. 'Darkling' involves a diminution of the faculty of seeing and an intensification of other faculties as if to (over)compensate. To be 'darkling' is to be gifted with an elevation of certain senses at the expense of others, and so represents a form of negative capability.

A more complicated, though not necessarily more satisfactory answer says that the 'Darkling' state in which he listens, which follows on from the perceived constraint on his faculties, includes those projections of metaphors, invisibilities and unsmellable smells alongside the auditory function which in any case he might possess 'in vain'; all these are varieties of near-nothingness. But this near-nothingness forms just enough of a mesh, finer than a spider's web, in which to catch the birdsong. To listen in a darkling state is to have that mesh placed across the ear and be sensitized to its vibrations. This makes 'darklingness' nothing less than the essence of what it is to be a poet. The true, authentic poet is one possessed of the darkling senses capable of printing the music of birdsong onto that weightless gauze. As I discussed in Chapter 4, on voice, there is a quintessentially poetical process that turns sound into image, or voice into light. To be sure, the 'light' here is a dark one, with the darkling operating as a kind of chemical compound or resin that fixes the image as if with henna on a shroud. But the effort to make the voice refulgent is the same. The extra complication being that

'voice' in this ode pertains to both that of the nightingale and that
of the poet, not that they are entirely separate: there is enough Ovid
garlanded around these lines for us to take it as almost axiomatic
that the poet's voice might metamorphose into that of the nightingale or vice versa, or has already done so.

A third reading goes as follows. To be 'darkling' is to have one's
faculties melted into a narcotic stew that might sharpen, but might
also stupefy them; and it is to realize that every high has an equal
and opposite low, a comedown so steep and bleak that thoughts of
suicide creep in. Yet such self-murder (I say 'self-murder' because
of so much Hamlet in 'Now more than ever seems it rich to die,/
To cease upon the midnight with no pain'), could still be 'rich'
if carried out at exactly the peak of the high, when the nightingale pipes the high C of its song. 'Darkling' now becomes not
just subjectivity's totem, but the verbal music that accompanies
a plunging sense of the self as mortal, as blighted with its own
darkling fate. The life of the subject will go dark, and as a present
participle the '-ling' suffix represents the living adumbration of that
end, the last quivering of a being about to be snuffed out.

I mentioned darkling's gothic quality: why does Keats save it for
this ode rather than jimmying it like a pane of stained glass into
the ostentatiously Gothic architecture of 'St Agnes' Eve'? One can
easily picture it there as a lozenge of opaque light. Perhaps because
it is too precious a word to be left in a building, just part of the
poem's stage-set; the opportunity it provides of naming the disposition of the true poet too rare. In which connection, its possibilities
as the quasi-clinical name of a pathology have to be exploited.
'Darkling' might be gothic, but if you listen hard enough to its use
in these lines, it is almost medical, as if in the back of his mind
Keats were concocting a scientific paper on a subject to be an early
forerunner of the psychological neurology practised by Freud's
great influence, Charcot. Some jangling of the nerves is implied,
and although that sounds gothic enough, Keats has transferred its
gothicism, again, from the object to the subject, from gothic cause
to gothic effect.

Tennyson (1850)

Risest thou thus, dim dawn, again,
    So loud with voices of the birds,
    So thick with lowings of the herds,
Day, when I lost the flower of men;

Who tremblest thro' thy darkling red
    On yon swoll'n brook that bubbles fast
    By meadows breathing of the past,
And woodlands holy to the dead;

Who murmurest in the foliaged eaves
    A song that slights the coming care,
    And Autumn laying here and there
A fiery finger on the leaves;

Who wakenest with thy balmy breath
    To myriads on the genial earth,
    Memories of bridal, or of birth,
And unto myriads more, of death.

O wheresoever those may be,
    Betwixt the slumber of the poles,
    To-day they count as kindred souls;
They know me not, but mourn with me.[3]

In the next chapter of this book I look in depth at another lyric from *In Memoriam*, known as 'Dark house'. Here I want to focus again exclusively on the use of 'darkling'. The word finds itself in what looks at first like grammatical limbo. In the opening line of the second stanza – 'Who tremblest thro' thy darkling red' – the 'Who' could plausibly refer back to any one of three subjects in the first – dawn, day or the flower of men (i.e. Hallam) – even 'I', just about. Such a limbo wouldn't be so inapposite: it would give the 'darkling red' an ethereal character, as if it were a gas wafting around all of those potential subjects, clothing them like ghosts. The ambiguity isn't quite removed by deciding, as seems sensible, that 'Day' is the object risen by the dawn, as in 'Dawn, do you rise/raise the day again, even though Hallam is dead and can't himself be risen? How dare you keep waking up the day when my beloved friend is lost? Especially as (a) it was on a 'day' that he died, and (b) every new day is therefore a reminder of that first day of my grief, the last day of my friend's life!' (I've added the rhetorical question mark, though its absence from the poem makes 'Risest thou' all the more solemn.) The poem could still be made to work if the recurrent 'Who' belongs to the day. Despite these possibilities, the '-est' endings of the verbs 'tremblest', 'murmurest', and so on, signify the second person singular, which had already been claimed by the 'thou' of dawn in the first line. This means that 'darkling red' would still apply to the dawn, as now would all those verbs, making the poem an extended apostrophe to that dawn. The sentiment would therefore run as follows: 'Dawn, you are so implacably raising the day again [...] despite my being in mourning; and are you trembling with a darkling red colour over that stream (whose vital surging is only another painful reminder of what I don't have).'

On this interpretation, 'darkling' takes on the following charac- teristics. First, it is a qualifier to 'red', making that red dark. As some of the examples quoted at the beginning of this chapter of other usages suggest, 'darkling' can be simply a more ornate way of saying 'dark', but without altering the meaning. Here, because the darkness of the dark red makes its appearance over a stream, we can see or hear in the '-ling' of the word some of the intermin- gling of the dawn air with the air above the water, a suggestion of a slight refraction through microscopic water particles, creating a soft sheen and a much-muted sparkle – not just darkness.

Secondly, the dawn's darkling red therefore takes on infinitesimal substance, like the quality of an impossibly sheer silk scarf on whose surface a 'trembling' can then be detected. With the rhyme later on of 'breath' and 'death', this trembling air that is a false intimation of Hallam's rising up again even suggests a momentary emission of air from the corpse's lips as it sleeps under its sheet, giving a (false again) hope of resurrection. Resurrection being the poem's organ- izing trope, as it realizes with a mixture of bitterness, consternation and awe that Hallam cannot be raised up again even if Christ and the dawn can. From this perspective (third point) the word 'darkling', as it hedges between the dead 'dark' and the living 'ling', marks the fact that death can go either way, slipping ever downwards into death's unreachable well or springing back to life. As such, the red worn by the darkling dawn has something of the colour of blood returning to once ghostly faces. Except, again, for that of Hallam (fourth point): the red sky in the morning is the mourner's warning that the new 'day' promises little more than waves of old memory. A darkling red is a cruel red because the curtain it pulls back, the curtain that 'rises', reveals only the natural progress of things, life going on as if indifferent to Tennyson's agony. Life goes on with such vigour, in fact, that the brook is 'swoll'n', the epithet used strikingly for sheep by Milton in 'Lycidas', the poem which is the key ancestor of Tennyson's. And, as in Milton, there is a touch of the grotesque in it, turning the 'darkling red' of the dawn into something slightly violent (fifth point). As in the famous 'nature red in tooth and claw', the red here, in combination with 'darkling' and 'swollen', half-creates the image of a contusion, the cruelty of dawn almost made graphic, and almost as if either Tennyson would blame the dawn itself for Hallam's death, or the 'darkling' refers indirectly to that death against which Tennyson, himself red with tears of anger, the blubber of grief, can only rail.

Arnold (1851)

Dover Beach

The sea is calm to-night.
The tide is full, the moon lies fair
Upon the straits;—on the French coast the light
Gleams and is gone; the cliffs of England stand,
Glimmering and vast, out in the tranquil bay.
Come to the window, sweet is the night-air!
Only, from the long line of spray
Where the sea meets the moon-blanch'd land,
Listen! You hear the grating roar
Of pebbles which the waves draw back, and fling,
At their return, up the high strand,
Begin, and cease, and then again begin,
With tremulous cadence slow, and bring
The eternal note of sadness in.

Sophocles long ago
Heard it on the Aegaean, and it brought
Into his mind the turbid ebb and flow
Of human misery; we
Find also in the sound a thought,
Hearing it by this distant northern sea.

The Sea of Faith
Was once, too, at the full, and round earth's shore
Lay like the folds of a bright girdle furl'd.
But now I only hear
Its melancholy, long, withdrawing roar,
Retreating, to the breath
Of the night-wind, down the vast edges drear
And naked shingles of the world.

Ah, love, let us be true
To one another! for the world, which seems
To lie before us like a land of dreams,
So various, so beautiful, so new,
Hath really neither joy, nor love, nor light,
Nor certitude, nor peace, nor help for pain;
And we are here as on a darkling plain
Swept with confused alarms of struggle and flight,
Where ignorant armies clash by night.[4]

The poem's celebrity might have more to do with its sentiment and
tone than its skill – it is probably too mannered a melee of poetical
tropes to count as 'great poetry'. But since the sentiment is partly
that of a courageous resourcefulness in the face of adversity, the
fact the poem itself plunders so many resources from literature
maybe carries its own vindication. Which is what keeps Arnold as
'literary' as he is 'poetic'. If Yeats was the last Romantic, Arnold
was the last neoclassicist, though writing at the high-water mark
of poeticism. A pathos of antiquity flows through the poem, which
the archaism of 'darkling' reflects.

   Here the word almost physically shuffles and adjusts time within
itself, and this is apt for a poem balanced on the apocalyptic cusp
of an era, on a fold in time. That is partly because the '-ling' suffix
seems to keep the word irresolutely strung between noun, adjective

and adverb. It is half thing, half movement, the word a tremor of largely suppressed anxiety. Far beneath its surface, in underground rivers, the poem courses with the adrenaline of chiliastic foreboding. It raises the spectre of putting time into reverse; the risk of a world turned upside down; a portentous eclipse; internecine warfare; the inversion of base and superior tribes. Figuring this correction in the world order, 'darkling' seems in the process of replacing itself, as if the consonants at its fabricky middle were pleated. The nap of the word is taken by the 'l' a little way back across the 'k', a partial eclipse or occlusion in accord with the word's signifying a darkness that nevertheless permits a tiny rustle of light to flash upwards from it. So any revelations, it seems to say, will be as dark as light, not completely revealed: 'darkling' has a sable shimmer; it is what remains on the page when you switch the lights off in the word 'sparkling'. It is a dark star.

The idea of being stationed out at the end of time, and the idea of being stationed out at the end of space, at the finisterre that is Dover beach, where land meets sea and sky: these joint ideas of temporal and spatial limit support each other. One travels to the limit in order to detect what is to come; change can be discerned at the margin before the centre. The vista there resembles the desert east of Eden, and it subverts the ideality of the lines preceding it, resonant as they are with Milton's Adam exhorting Eve (which picks up in turn the tragic unloosing of the girdle and nakedness of the previous stanza). The tragic couple glimpses the fallen life to come, 'darkling' now connoting the inkling or squinting intelligence of the future. The darkling plain even stretches back to before Eden, to the unformed dark waters of Genesis over which the spirit of God hovers like a vapour. In keeping with the faintly Homeric style, 'darkling' might in any case apply as well to water as land: 'the darkling sea' a re-expression of the 'wine-dark sea', the low complement to the high sparkling stars by which one might navigate it.

While the image of the spirit on the waters takes us back to an earlier origin than even Eden, it does so without reaching resolution or making the recalibration it might have hoped for. As a result, the spirit that ventures to this cultural palimpsest of a place stands bold, stoical, scientific, exploratory, defensive, colonial. As well as the more contemplative virtues that the poem urges on its reader, it encourages all these active attributes. In this context 'darkling' represents the test of those attributes represented by southern countries and, connected as it is with images of warring clans, gets associated with a certain primitivism, that of 'ignorant armies'. In keeping with a conventional prejudice, Greek culture is idealized at the expense of these neighbouring, 'darkling' cultures. Though idealized, however, Greek culture is equally exploited, Sophocles roped in at the service of what would have been to him a very foreign, imperialistic cause. It is as if the Greeks are thought of as having skin white as alabaster simply because of the colour of the sculpture embodying them, and there is nothing darkling about Sophocles here. The 'darkling plain' conjures up a post-diluvian landscape, the 'ark' discernible at the centre of the darkling plain accommodating only specially selected cultures and genealogies. In this light the lines 'Ah, love, let us be true/ To one another', with their pledge of fidelity, can be understood as being made in the shadow of the chaotic miscegenation that warfare heralds, of a fearful epoch when demographies alter, and exodus across the plain gets under way in vast legions looking from a distance like armies of insects – 'darkling' having a beetling blackness to it. The prophetic poet witnesses in his mind's eye the lustrous proliferation of swarming forces, armoured and chitinous like insects, the word 'darkling' clinking and sliding and grating against itself like panels of the body. When you first look you miss it, but when you look again you see teeming phalanxes, as 'darkling' articulates itself in a vast mat of black beads across the land, million-eyed and chthonic. You see it with second sight, when the eyes have become accustomed to the new darkness, and with the second sight of a prophecy of doom. The plague of chaos approaches with ineluc-table order, and the task is to prepare.

The protean capacity to appear to change form that the word 'darkling' has, attributable in part to the way the light falls on it, and which complements so well the dread of revolution that gnaws the edges of the poem, derives in part from the more generic sense borne by the '-ling' suffix. As in 'changeling', this word-ending hints at mutation or genetic distortion, a damned metamorphosis as suggested by, say, a bastard child or a 'foundling'. What was for so long secure becomes subject to change, to being changed, broken down, exchanged, hived off, and replaced with newcomers who are at best semi-legitimate, at worst false copies or imper-sonators of those they supplant. As such, 'darkling' bristles with an uncanniness beckoning strange forms forward in its dun afterglow, what in Freudian terms would be the 'return of the repressed', the coming to light of what should have remained hidden.

Hardy (1900)

The Darkling Thrush

I leant upon a coppice gate
    When Frost was spectre-gray,
And Winter's dregs made desolate
    The weakening eye of day.
The tangled bine-stems scored the sky
    Like strings of broken lyres,
And all mankind that haunted nigh
    Had sought their household fires.

The land's sharp features seemed to be
    The Century's corpse outleant,
His crypt the cloudy canopy,
    The wind his death-lament.
The ancient pulse of germ and birth
    Was shrunken hard and dry,
And every spirit upon earth
    Seemed fervourless as I.

At once a voice arose among
    The bleak twigs overhead
In a full-hearted evensong
    Of joy illimited;
An aged thrush, frail, gaunt, and small,
    In blast-beruffled plume,
Had chosen thus to fling his soul
    Upon the growing gloom.

So little cause for carolings
    Of such ecstatic sound
Was written on terrestrial things

Afar or nigh around,
That I could think there trembled through
    His happy good-night air
Some blessed Hope, whereof he knew
    And I was unaware.

31 December 1900[5]

That by the year 1900 the word 'darkling' can be used in a title
suggests it is copper-bottomed – even if, therefore, its 'poetic' status
has begun to tarnish. With the seal of approval given it by not
just Shakespeare and Milton, but also Keats, Tennyson, Arnold,
Browning, Barrett Browning, Byron, etc. the word signals literary
authority itself, and that is partly why it can be hoisted to the
heights of a title. The accrual of literary authority to the word,
however, makes it deeper and shallower at once: deeper because of
the allusions encrusted about it; shallower because the same process
causes a muffling, rendering it more ordinary, less surprising. The
pang of alarm that 'darkling' caused in 'Dover Beach' owed in
part to a *comparative* novelty; in Keats, the dark surprise was the
presence of the word itself as much as what it denoted.

To offset this erosion of the word, Hardy has time on his side.
As in Arnold, Hardy's 'Darkling' rings an apocalyptic, if less
pessimistic, knell, but the timely use of it at the century's end, 31
December 1900, gives it special resonance. In case we miss this
fact, the date is printed at the bottom, like a big fat clue. (There
may be some confusion here: we generally think of the end of a
century as ending in the year 99. Strictly speaking, and according
to the custom of Hardy's day, the century ends a year later. The first
year of this century was 2001, not 2000.) Now, this century-speak
or century-think is pervasive. One thinks in centuries like one
thinks in decimal units: a binary system, say, would be eccentric.
What began as a convenient, if arbitrary, means of classification
ends as an apparently natural segmentation of history, as if
historical rhythms really did pause once a unit of ten or a hundred
years had been clocked up. One even acts 'as if': as if between the
end of 31 December and the beginning of 1 January much more
than a nanosecond passes, whereas a date, in its arbitrariness, is
technically as 'fictional' as anything in a poem marked with this
(or any) date stamp. So although we are invited to marvel at the

convergence of a literary event (the poem) with a factual event (the end of the century), the latter is to an extent compromised by an imaginary element. What is more, the caesura marked by the date between one century and the next is itself a limit between reality and fiction: the next century is a fiction because it lies in the future, existing solely in our imagination. In sum, a date is a 'fictional' (arbitrary) bookmark between a real now and fictional future, and when it is included in a *poem*, itself a 'fictional' form, the fictionality is redoubled.

What is the consequence for the word 'darkling'? Because it sits in the title, it both does and doesn't belong to the poem. A title forms a shelf along the top of a poem that backs onto reality, so to speak, because as the 'name' of a poem it will appear in bibliographies, indexes and tables of contents, a fact which lends the title of a poem a quantum of reality not so accessible to the poem's main body. 'Darkling' – once so poetic, now so literary – acquires some of its premonitory force from being located in this, the title's proud corner of reality. Placed in a title, Hardy's 'darkling' assumes a prophetic credibility greater than that when studded into the stanzas of 'Dover Beach'. Up to a point, this reality is even ratified by the date stamp in so far as the latter reaches out into the real world. But because, as I have said, a date never quite gets beyond being 'fictional', the reality thus given to 'darkling' is at once reduced. This is why the word feels both paramount in its earnestness and the tiniest bit fake; it is only a poet's take on future events – prophetic but also speculative, aesthetic and affected. As such, it combines a real if unevidenced announcement of the shape of things to come, and a fantasy whose appeal stems from the fact that the word has become literary. To use the word 'darkling' is to pretend insight into the future that is based on little more than the word's associations.

As if to see into things properly, what is required is not, as Goethe is said to have demanded on his deathbed, '*mehr licht*' ('more light'), but the opposite. Poetic seeing needs the lights to be turned down a little, the light of reason being too harsh, too crude, too fascist. If I have said that poetic voice dreams of becoming light, I should add that that light, even at its most radiant, must absorb into it a certain darkness that better allows things to be discerned.

7

Forgetting Tennyson's memory

Dark house, by which once more I stand
  Here in the long unlovely street,
  Doors, where my heart was used to beat
So quickly, waiting for a hand,

A hand that can be clasp'd no more—
  Behold me, for I cannot sleep,
  And like a guilty thing I creep
At earliest morning to the door.

He is not here; but far away
  The noise of life begins again,
  And ghastly thro' the drizzling rain
On the bald street breaks the blank day.[1]

Before diving into the verses of this lyric – which I consider, along with, say, 'Royal Fern' by J. H. Prynne, among the greatest in the English language – I will put them into wider context. The title *In Memoriam* – by which Tennyson's series of 131 lyrics plus a prologue and epilogue, composed in the 1830s and 1840s, is commonly known – is an aposiopesis, a phrase cut short. Obscured by the Latin, which looks and sounds complete, its incompleteness becomes obvious when translated into the English: 'In memory of'.

In memory of whom? one now wants to know. Of Arthur Henry
Hallam, Tennyson's dear friend who died at the age of 27. The full
title should read 'In Memoriam A. H. H.' But even with the 'A.
H. H.' added, the title remains incomplete, partly because 'A. H.
H.' is itself an abbreviation; partly because there is a subtitle, 'The
Way of the Soul'; and partly because title and subtitle are, like 'The
Darkling Thrush' which I looked at earlier, accompanied by a date,
'OBIT MDCCCXXXIII' (1833), the date of death.

These facts about Tennyson's title, which seem merely bibliographical, are not incidental to the poem's elegiac purpose. *In
Memoriam* is not so much a title as a statement of that purpose, of
why the poem has been written: it announces that these 131+ lyrics
have been written to commemorate Hallam. Had the subtitle, 'The
Way of the Soul', been the main title, it would have been a different
matter – the words 'In Memoriam A. H. H.' could then have been
added as a dedication. Except that using the phrase 'In Memoriam
A. H. H.' as a dedication would diminish its status relative not
only to a title but to the magnitude of Hallam's passing. In the
wake of that passing and its colossal metaphysical import, all titles
look too worldly, too trivial. How best anyway to recognize the
dead, especially a dead person with whom we were/are obsessively
in love? That the commemorative dedication 'In Memoriam A. H.
H.' has been promoted to the title of this magnum opus is good;
that in so doing, some of that dedicatory intent has been wiped, not
so good. What is worse, its becoming a title has led to the phrase
'In Memoriam A. H. H.' getting abbreviated to 'In Memoriam', a
process of popularization or degradation in which the whole point
of its becoming a title – the naming and honouring of Hallam –
has been somewhat lost. Today we call it *In Memoriam* and thus
tend to forget rather than remember A. H. H. in whose memory
it was written. The grief was Tennyson's back then, not ours now.
We readers, in all our innocence, are free of mourning. We are just
spectators on Tennyson's terrible grief.

If the Latinity of the dedication-become-title *In Memoriam* lends
antiquity and gravitas to the titular apparatus, then the subtitle,
'The Way of the Soul', both concentrates and dilutes it. It has a
solemn enough ring, but not only is it in English as opposed to
Latin, it brings a pagan or para-religious or pre-religious twist.
'Soul' is more diffuse, ecumenical and 'oriental' than 'spirit' would
have been, and the concept of metempsychosis implicit in a 'way'

of the soul points either eastwards to Hinduism and Buddhism, or in the general direction of theosophy, or both, and certainly beyond what is sometimes taken to be the poem's otherwise unimpeachable Christianity (Tennyson's prologue opens with 'Strong Son of God'). This complicates the much-invoked antagonism between Christianity and Darwinism, of which Lord Tennyson was to become so hardy a symbol: as 'The Way of the Soul' hints, he can even be thought of in the Victorian ghost-story tradition. As we'll see in 'Dark house', these intertwining religious, paranormal and mystic strands hardly get less entwined as we study them.

The notion of Hallam's soul being swept like stardust up into an imperceptible cosmic journey opens up a second time dimension in the poem. The first is the ordinary time in which Tennyson, man, mourner and poet, finds himself. It involves the phases of mourning, the beats of the grieving heart, the rhythm of funeral rites, the rituals of memorial observance, the circularity of anniversaries, and the wider periodicity of human life as it carries on. This time is fixed in tabular form in the words 'In Memoriam', which in conjunction with the numerals in 'MDCCCXXXIII' point to the metrics of datable time. The time of the soul operates on an altogether different rhythm, a time outside memory. While the human animal might remember everything from his or her own lifetime, including the life and death of a friend, that friend's existence reaches into margins stretching far beyond. Hallam's life as known by Tennyson was a mere dot in the soul's sequence. How does *In Memoriam* fit with these two time schemes, worldly and unworldly? While the lyrics that make up the anthology *In Memoriam* are at one level neat and tidy, they are also irregular, compendious, open-ended, episodic, half-resumptive. These features appear to defy, resist or disrupt the regular time of quotidian life in order to draw attention to Hallam's absence. It is as if by breaking out of the first time dimension, they hope to tune into the second. The arrhythmia of the 131+ piece oeuvre as a whole serves to spread Tennyson's bets, in the hope of tearing a rent in ordinary time through which Hallam's soul might just, if only briefly, reappear, like a figure at the heart of one of Turner's late gold-and-white canvases.

Not that that concerns us, the reader. As I was saying, we need make no mourning, being free merely to read, read and be free, where reading in this context implies non-responsibility. We readers are even invested in Hallam's soul *not* returning, its staying away serving as the work's condition of possibility. Consider, however, these Derridean questions: Is Hallam's absence really so necessary? Did Hallam need to die for Tennyson to write his elegy? Could Tennyson have written his elegy for Hallam before Hallam died? Just as newspapers will sometimes assemble material for an obituary before the death of the subject, so a poet can put together an elegy before its subject's demise. Textually speaking, such actions do nothing to vitiate the poem and its requirements – praising the subject, remembering key events, commenting on his or her traits. The fact the subject is not yet dead doesn't mar the content as such, even if drafting the elegy of a living person might be tactless or morbid. This possibility of the 'premature elegy' derives from the fact that we can bear people in our hearts and minds whether they are dead or alive; there is nothing that transpires at the moment of death to change this ability. In so far as the name and the mental effigy of Hallam had long installed themselves in his faithful mind, Tennyson was already in mourning, and the phrase 'In Memoriam' records a state prevailing before 1833.

From this perspective, the primordial distinction between life and death loses some – though not all – of its edge. Hallam may continue to occupy Tennyson's mind, just as he had before death, but his body has gone, and with it the possibility of any response from him. It may be true that Tennyson, like some of his Victorian peers, had a taste for seances, and who knows what contact was made, but as far as an elegy is concerned, it sits in silence. An elegy may call out to the deceased, may even try to recreate his voice, but it never hears anything in response, making the genre one of infinite patience. Unless *In Memoriam* is not an elegy. Most elegies look back on the life of the subject, closure having been achieved beforehand or effected by the writing of the poem itself; *In Memoriam,* by contrast, shows an unresting working-through that never quite seems to work anything through, getting stuck in the ruts of the grieving mind only to turn violently in circles, trying to get out. Perhaps it is best classified as threnody, bearing in mind the root of this term in the notion of wailing – lamentation without solace or relief. Whatever genre it is, the work becomes a cave of its own echoes, as torturing no doubt as it was for Tennyson to remain inside his own head after his friend's death. I use the image of the cave expressly to recall Plato and the loss of the ideal form, in this case represented by (the irrevocable) Hallam. Within it, there is not even the certainty that *In Memoriam* concerns Hallam, for to the extent that neither requires the presence of a living being, mourning has merged with imagination. On the contrary, it is with the departure of what they imagine or mourn that they commence. Both mourning and imagination transplant the empirically invisible (the dead Hallam) to stand visibly before the mind's eye. But what stands is only an image, not the thing in itself. Hallam wasn't fictional, but he would have been hosted in Tennyson's memory in much the same way fictional characters would have been, like Maud or the Lady of Shallott.

In 'Dark house', even the image threatens to not show up. The disconsolate final line, 'On the bald street breaks the blank day', confirms that when dawn rises and real things gather into position like a congregation out of the fog, or like actors on a stage, nothing appears to me, Tennyson. The light is blank. Which is absurdly true, for light is white and paradoxically invisible. Light, the condition of visibility, is invisible, characterless, blank. In 'breaks the blank', what breaks is nothing; what appears, parodying a ghost, is what doesn't appear. The bleakness of 'breaks the blank' emphasizes the lack of light in this mute clay-like light, a light more like death because the only life that matters to Tennyson remains on the other side.

The effect is to make life death, and so turn all the values inside out. The pallor of this life is deathly because it is not death, death being where Hallam lives, making the death-world the world of life. This world, the one on this side, is the ghost of its former self, blanked out and enervated. In turn, Tennyson himself becomes a ghost, sleepwalking with the skull-like tomb that is his memory through the ghostlike world that is both too real and entirely insubstantial. Behind 'breaks the blank' one even hears 'breaks the bank'. Without Hallam the human world is bankrupt, the odds are gone, and the possibility of redemption beyond reach. This is Hallam as banker of Tennyson's soul, the only one who could bail him out, while Tennyson, 'waiting for a hand', remains empty-handed.

The mocking flatness of 'breaks the blank' very faintly echoes the insomniac's blanket, untouched and unbroken for the whole of the night at the point when Tennyson shuffles into the chalk-pale dawn. The 'blank day' stares back at the unblinking zombie Tennyson has become, as he assumes the automatic actions of the waking dead – the waking of the dead being his hope for Hallam. Not to sleep is not to have died properly: sleep is death's second self, so with a further reversal it is the unsleeping mourner, rather than the deceased, who is the one in limbo. Even suicide, for the Christian poet, is not an option – the blank connoting the suicide's pistol that cannot be made to fire – leaving nothing to break the blankness, no means of blowing a hole through to the other side. And so he trudges on.

The one advantage of this insomniac existence is that it nearly boards the second time dimension I mentioned above, that of the soul, which knows no measure. The sleepless vigil for the dead imitates the sleeping dead in so far as the latter have flitted away to join the dateless, measureless time of the soul. This attenuated fluid spiritual rhythm is then juddered and jolted by the diurnal time that rumbles like a bass drum through the 'b' sounds – beats of the heart, beats on the door, breaking of the blank dawn – all false to one obsessed with latching on to the time of the soul that remains out of reach. The beats of the heart remind us that the heart itself is a mnemonic, keeping measure like the beats of a line. It recalls mortality, each beat counting down the beats allotted to us. From this perspective, the word 'bald' refers both ironically to the youthfulness of the dead man whose measure has expired, and mercilessly to the ageing of his surviving brother. Hallam, freed from time, becomes a clock in Tennyson's heart.

As the clock winds down, the heart beating a retreat along the street, the image of the hand that cannot be grasped becomes all the more poignant. The waiting at the door for a hand that never joins his takes us straight into Tennyson's fantasy as a groom or bride jilted at a wedding. Locked up inside this nuptial imagery, which appears elsewhere in *In Memoriam* – not least the epilogue that celebrates the wedding of Tennyson's sister – are several tropes. Most obvious is the homoerotic. A 'guilty thing', Tennyson is the lover creeping 'at earliest morning to the door' to slip out before the house awakes, himself having not slept but made love all night, his heart beating fast, in a dark house. Belonging to this erotic trope is the word 'hand', the breath quickening with the repeated 'h', and the effect it has on the word 'Behold':

> Doors, where my heart was used to beat
> So quickly, waiting for a hand,

A hand that can be clasp'd no more—
Behold me, for I cannot sleep

The hand, clasped, turns 'Behold me' into 'Hold me' – the preceding two 'h' sounds grasping for the third, overlooking the 'Be-'. Like a bride in her husband's hands, she or he is saying 'hold me for I cannot sleep, protect me, give me comfort'.

The associations of the cancelled wedding spread further. Here is Tennyson, practising his private ('home-made' as Eliot would call it)[2] religion of mourning, and if the guilt comes partly from shame at his homosexual feelings, it comes also from their relationship to Christianity, though not on the usual grounds that homosexuality is an un-Christian activity. The church is the bride of Christ (Christ's birth at Christmas is already set against Hallam's death), but when Tennyson finds himself at church door, his knock unanswered, he confuses the two, Hallam and Christ. As if they were somehow comparable! Hallam may be a paragon, as the dead should be, but because only human his exemplarity cannot but be qualified and superseded by Christ. The *sui generis* 'example' of Christ tempers the human desire to identify too much with other humans, frowning on these private elegies. Being a poet, Tennyson can't help mixing things up, seeing reality as metaphor and vice versa, even to the point of confusing Christ with Hallam, while the very figure of Christ, in its pre-eminence, wants to outlaw substitutions, especially of himself. For poets tend to work by metaphor and substitution, whereas Christianity, so brotherly a religion, so indulgent at one level of those who wish to imitate Christ or join together like Tennyson and Hallam as brothers in Christ, also insists that Christ can have no substitute, and that those, like poets, who trade in substitutions, might indeed be guilty things. Substitution is the devil's work. Hallam, so Christ wants to say, has died, gone to heaven, and become a 'bride' of Christ, like the church: he belongs to me now. You, Tennyson, need to remember that. You can be brother disciples, because fraternity at that level is right and proper, but disciples only of me, not each other. What is more, you need to make a separation. Hallam was your divine fantasy: it's me who is the reality, the truth, the light.

Meanwhile, Tennyson can't stop pulling back to the earthly: the debasement that makes him creep remains all too human, so that the 'Ecce homo' that declares 'Behold Christ' is translated as merely 'Behold me'. Barely human, indeed, more like a faithful dog creeping to the door for its absent master to feed it, standing vigil by its master's grave in the hope of some earthbound miracle. The fidelity is excessive and misdirected. What is worse, according to the book of Christian errors, is that this human propensity for substitutions, for literature and imagination, can become so theatrical, and that Christ himself could be mistaken for some *deus ex machina*. Again, however, the theatrical potential doesn't materialize, and Tennyson fails to put on a show; the image, whether Hallam or Christ, remains in the wings. This is because 'Dark house' refers to the closure of theatres, owing to censorship or disease, dark days in either case, and the suppression of amusements, the loss of fantasy. The theatrical trope also accounts for the foreshortened scale in 'Dark house, by which once more I stand', for standing 'by' a house, rather than in front of it or before it, has the effect of shrinking it, as if it were a replica, a scale model, a toy theatre. 'Waiting for a hand' would then also be waiting for applause that never comes, or for a puppeteer who fails to turn up for the event, despite appearing on the bill.

On therefore to the second 'sin', that of nihilism, best expressed again in the fathomless despair of 'On the bald street breaks the blank day'. Hallam and Christ might have got confused, but the interminable and enervating ageing of the 'bald street' suggests there will be no second coming for either. Instead, the street leads to the bad rather than the good eternity, more wretched in its mediocrity than the hell that at least has heat to burn the blankness away, like the silver of a photograph in the 'dark house' that nearly translates *camera obscura*. The heart keeps breaking without breaking, its sinewy, strained nervousness contained in the neurasthenia of the 'str' in 'street'. The double 'e' of street marks out the long trajectory of Tennyson's death march, buffeted on either side by 'bald' and 'breaks'. The 'guilty thing' who picks up a candle from both Macbeth and Hamlet looks numbly ahead to 'Tomorrow and tomorrow and tomorrow', and the rest continues to be silence or emptiness, cruelly exacerbated by the anti-comfort of placing 'He is not here' together with 'but far away' while severing them with a semi-colon.

Unredeemable, perhaps, but the nihilism is not quite complete. Apart from the admittedly negative energy of Tennyson's repetition compulsion that keeps him masochistically coming back for more (i.e. less), there is a profound stoicism. Private though his grief may be, it is entangled not only with that public Christianity and the risk of defaulting on it, but also with a soldierliness. As guilty, Tennyson resembles an army deserter bewildered and hesitant in the civilian street; but as faithful, he is the loyal husband come back from the war to claim the bride he did and didn't possess, the hand still waiting; and as released from his relationship with Hallam, he is the soldier discharged from the army after peace has been declared, entirely at a loss as to what to do next, but prepared to make the best of it. Should he simply 'stand' like a sentry, marking his 'beat', at least imitating, like a security guard, the military life in the new decommissioned context?

I mentioned Tennyson's repetition compulsion. It's not just that of the mourner who keeps returning to the shrine. Nor that of the child in the middle verse creeping out of bed thanks to a recurrent nightmare, saying hold me, for I cannot sleep, and the guilt of getting up in the night and breaking the Victorian house rules. Repetition compulsion also defines elegy per se – or threnody, to use my earlier distinction. The 'once more' in 'Dark house, by which once more I stand' recalls Milton's 'Yet once more, O ye laurels, and once more/ Ye myrtles brown …', expressing the resurgence of grief, the return that makes revenants appear.[3] True mourning believes it will never end – it is an experience of infinity, if that's not a contra-diction in terms. After all, mourning that foresees a finishing line wouldn't be mourning but a formulaic gesture; to say 'I'll grieve for n months' is not to grieve at all, for what is grievous about grief is its limitlessness – even if that requires, strangely, the mourner's immortality (it is only by living for ever that one can properly mourn for the dead). Hence again that irregular number of lyrics, 131, leaving the door open for more mourning, mourning flooding into everything that tries to come after and organize it. And yet as a threnody/elegy, *In Memoriam* also commemorates previous elegiac works like 'Lycidas' – especially 'Lycidas', in fact. Which means that, like it or not, there is some polluting of Tennyson's own grief, some brake on that endlessness. Remember this is a poem written from within a literary tradition; it is not an unvarnished expression of grief by one man for another, assuming such a thing were ever possible. Forgetting the obvious point that elegies are often 'narcis-sistic', often as much about the writer as their subject, 'Dark house' is written with the knowledge of another man's grief, Milton's for Edward King, and, more to the point, with the knowledge of Milton's poesy, his formal articulation of that grief. The infinity of mourning, in this respect, is heavily circumscribed. It refers to the incorporation of *literary* elements into the mourning, over and above the fact that an elegy/threnody was already literary and therefore at risk of appearing too factitious for the mourning task it purports to enact. When, however unwittingly, Tennyson uses the phrase 'once more', it switches on, like a string of lights, a history of artifice; it even names it, in so far as 'once more' also says 'once more I use the phrase "once more"'. The problem is analogous to that of scripture containing literary elements: shouldn't grief, like religion, be purified of such inventions? Don't they corrupt it?

In turn, 'Dark house' is looked back on. I am thinking of Philip Larkin's 'Aubade', which I'd go so far as to say is a rewriting of Tennyson's lyric.[4] There is the insomniac 'Waking at four to soundless dark I stare'; the 'blank' in 'The mind blanks at the glare'; the dreaded spectre of the day beginning again in 'world begins to rouse'; the idea of interminable, ominous knocking on doors in 'Postmen like doctors go from house to house'; and so on. The difference is that Larkin's is expressly an imaginary mourning, grieving without kin to grieve for, looking ahead to his own death rather than backwards towards that of another. Perhaps that says something about the difference between twentieth-century poetry and what precedes it. Where Tennyson mourns the loss of Hallam, Larkin mourns the loss of anything to grieve except the self in all its mistaken freedom.

A few last notes on 'Dark house':

Dark house, by which once more I stand: the dark is low, but the I is high, reinforced by 'stand', which also suggest taking up a soap-box on a street corner, in order to deliver an albeit deranged homily; there's also the suggestion of taking the stand in order to bear witness, reinforced in turn by the notion of 'standing by' a statement in the sense of vouching for its truth, as well as that of being 'on standby', ready to be summoned.

Here in the long unlovely street,: a somewhat melodramatic, even camp phrase; notice the 'e' sights and sounds, serving to make the whole line as lateral as possible, while the 'l' sounds in 'long unlovely' try unsuccessfully to untie themselves from each other as if loping three-leggedly down that street.

Doors, where my heart was used to beat: the first word 'Doors' is a beat on the line as denoted by the line's last word. There is also the strange image of Tennyson's heart itself beating on the door, as if it had reached ahead of the hand, so urgent is its mission.

So quickly, waiting for a hand: a shorter line, hence 'so quickly', it contains the wartime paradox of 'hurry up and wait'.

A hand that can be clasp'd no more— : the dash indicates a gesture of the hand that acts out the first two words of the line; the clasp suggests a token of remembrance.

Behold me, for I cannot sleep,: the double consonant in 'cannot' serves as a marker of resistance.

And like a guilty thing I creep: the 'gu' of 'guilty' disappears down the throat as if spoken by an animal that creeps with its larynx set back.

At earliest morning to the door.: there is a crispness in 'earliest', which brings a freshness to an otherwise funereal lyric, suggesting matins rather than prayers for the dead (morning rather than mourning).

He is not here; but far away: the line is effectively all preposition, in that 'here' and 'far away' are abstractions without content; the line is a false antithesis because the 'far away' points to the next line, not back to the first hemistich. Gray's elegy is echoed too ('Far from the madding crowd's ignoble strife') – it's not all 'Lycidas'!

The noise of life begins again,: the two 's' sounds are actually 'z' sounds, suggesting a buzz or a hum that won't achieve the piercing vitality that real 's' sounds would have made.

And ghastly thro' the drizzling rain: 'ghastly' obviously refers to 'ghostly' and the wider confusion between the Christian Holy Ghost and the return, or not, of Hallam.

On the bald street breaks the blank day.: the 'day' is merciless; that is what a day is, breaking like a wave only to retreat and break again, endlessly, never washing any sign of life to the shore.

8

Hopkins, 'f' and 'l'

I want to read Gerard Manley Hopkins through the filter of two letters so compulsively combined by him that they seem to fly to each other like iron filings under a magnet. They are 'f' and 'l'. Here are some examples, with italics added:

It will *flame* out, like shining from shook *foil*
('God's Grandeur')[1]

As kingfishers catch fire, dragon*flies* draw *flame*
('As kingfishers catch fire')[2]

Flesh fade, and mortal trash
Fall to the residuary worm; | world's *wildfire*, leave but ash:
    In a *flash*
('That Nature is a Heraclitean Fire')[3]

[…] me frantic to avoid thee and *flee*?

    Why? That my chaff might *fly*;
('Carrion Comfort')[4]

Rural, rural keeping — *folk*, *flocks*, and *flowers*
('Duns Scotus's Oxford')[5]

And *fled* with a *fling* of the heart to the heart of the Host.
[…]
To *flash* from the *flame* to the *flame* then
('The Wreck of the Deutschland')[6]

Not that the sweet-*fowl*, song-*fowl*, needs no rest —
[...]
Man's spirit will be *flesh*-bound
('The Caged Skylark')[7]

Felix Randal the farrier, O is he dead then?
[...]
Fatal four disorders, *fleshed* there
('Felix Randal')[8]

   cliffs of *fall*
Frightful, sheer, no-man-fathomed
('No worst, there is none.')[9]

Felled and *furled* them, the hearts of oak!
   And *flockbells* off the aerial
Downs' *forefalls*
('The Loss of the Eurydice')[10]

If you like, this pairing of 'f' and 'l' vocables can be read as the
insignia of the phrase 'faith in language'. For who more than
Hopkins exhibits a faith in language as fierce, if it is remotely
comparable, as his faith in God?

Well, the two are comparable *if only* because the duress to which
Hopkins subjects his language exists to maximize the torsion, the
tensile presence, that is God's signature in the world, and that corre-
sponds to a mortal tightening of the strings – musical strings, heart
strings, the strings of strained prayer – almost to the point of snapping.

Yet because Hopkins' faith in language is so aggressive, one
cannot help wondering whether it is less secure than it seems.
Just as the sonnet on carrion comfort highlights the temptation of
despair, so the blacksmith intensity with which he works his inflec-
tions suggests he is deeply worried that they won't do the job, that
they will fail to reflect the divine wonder so immanent around him.
Both his faith in language and his faith in God creep along a ridge
with a sheer drop.

Now, if God were visible, there would be no need for faith. He would
be revealed for all to see, and faith would be replaced by knowledge.
Not seeing is believing, yet in Hopkins, possessed of a religious faith
at once so ardent and so shakeable, we find an extraordinary emphasis

not only on the visible, but on a kind of super-visibility. Instead of faith as faith in what cannot be seen, faith becomes enhanced, even to the point of rapturous frenzy, by the visible. He is desperate to see God, if not directly then by the evidence of nature which he details so passionately in notebooks, letters and poems. The abundant specificity of life-forms confirms the sparkling presence of God as if he had been smashed like a diamond across the earth.

So there is a play between visible and invisible, two terms that represent and also complement the play in turn between faith and doubt – with the proviso that the stakes of this 'play' are deadly serious. The relationship between visible, invisible, faith, and doubt and the capacity in turn of language to faithfully reflect that relationship creates the obsession in Hopkins with the membranous, fretted interstice between God and mortal, a crossing-point that those two letters, 'f' and 'l', are designed to mark out. Take the lines just quoted from 'That Nature is a Heraclitean Fire':

> *Flesh* fade, and mortal trash
> *Fall* to the residuary worm; | world's *wildfire*, leave but ash:
>   In a *flash*

The spring in the 'fl' of 'Flesh' serves to pull and bend the word as if it were elasticated sinews of the body: the racking involved stretches the flesh to the point at which its mortality becomes as visible, as painfully exposed, as it would under dissection. What gathers upon this vulnerable mortal frame, thus stretched, is the parasite of the 'worm' and the spodogenous residue of 'ash', both of which speak to an abrupt loss of redeeming faith, leaving anything metaphysical to be consumed by the physical in a 'flash'. But the 'fl' of 'flash' points to an incandescent, cosmic energy – that of Heraclitean fire – which like the Big Bang predated everything and contained the atoms from which that body was fashioned. Its life force is immeasurable, and though the splicing together of pre-Socratic thought with Christian faith will always raise questions, their combined power, as compressed in this 'flash', easily offsets the deathliness. Thus the word 'flash' becomes a four-pointed star, with doubt, faith, life and death in each corner, its flame so bright that it is visible and invisible at the same time.

If, however, the star metaphor implies that each of the four elements (doubt, faith, life, death) could remain separate, it is misleading. What the 'fl' in both 'Flesh' and 'flash' denotes is an essential tension that binds competing, even opposing forces, and risks explosion. It is about a necessary frettedness that elsewhere Hopkins describes as 'dappled' or 'pied' – 'fl' words themselves being dappled in so far as the 'f' and the 'l' flick across each other. To use Saussurean language, it is the relationship *between* elements that matters, rather than any element in itself. Go back to the example from 'God's Grandeur':

It will *flame* out, like shining from shook *foil*

'Shook foil' agitates a million scintillas of light to clash together from different points, thus producing the 'flame' whose plume depends on momentarily binding together volatile energies that might otherwise become fissiparous. The 'fl' makes of these fiery elements a coil ready to be sprung, insisting on pulling them together.

As in the 'flash', this 'flame' derives some of its thrilling impact from not being anticipated. Though the forces bound together by Hopkins in his use of 'f' and 'l' sounds cannot extricate themselves from each other, the volatile compound that they make is such that it could detonate at any point, no one knows when. 'Fl', in other words, is also the sign of chance. What is more, there is a link between chance and permutation, between chance and the combining of letters such as 'f' and 'l', because chance is nothing if not the condition under which two elements, such as two letters, might collide with one another. And it is the coming together of things at an irregular angle and at an unforeseen moment – in a cross-weaving, trellised, or latticed pattern – that dapples to produce what Hopkins celebrates as 'pied' phenomena like the shapes of clouds, or the mottled shadows cast by leaves. The flecked relation between patches of light and dark depend on moment-to-moment recombinations that cannot be forecast.

Chance even provides one of the few frames through which pre-Socratic and Christian thinking appear to share common ground, for in Hopkins' febrile theology, both thought-systems conceive a firmament drenched with divinity from which 'God' will only randomly appear, like the miraculous apparition of a windhover. The combustion of the elements in Heraclitus, say, just cannot be predicted, but it is worth waiting for because when it does it sears the mind; Christ reveals himself on a similar basis, as the chance interpellation from a divine infinity that the human eye, for all its watchfulness, struggles to detect. The nexus of 'f' and 'l' is charged with enacting the flinging of divine force into the world, as aleatory, rare and ephemeral as a comet. If there is a supernatural darkness that hangs like a vast black brocade across the back of Hopkins' poetry, its opacity serves both to conceal the approach of the divine as well as to make it stand out all the more when it flies earthwards, making the brocade itself a kind of 'shook foil'.

Not only does chance help make sense of the religious sensibility suggested in Hopkins' poetry, it also accounts in part for Hopkins' aesthetics. On the grounds that what is beautiful is good, and what is good is godly? Yes, and glory be to God especially for dappled things. Glory be to dappled things too for being so beautiful – a sentiment made obvious by the phrase 'pied beauty' and the poem it names:[11]

GLORY be to God for dappled things—
　　For skies of couple-colour as a brinded cow;
　　　　For rose-moles all in stipple upon trout that swim;
Fresh-firecoal chestnut-falls; finches' wings;
　　Landscape plotted and pieced—fold, fallow, and plough;
　　　　And áll trádes, their gear and tackle and trim.

All things counter, original, spare, strange;
　　Whatever is fickle, freckled (who knows how?)
　　　　With swift, slow; sweet, sour; adazzle, dim;
He fathers-forth whose beauty is past change:
　　　　Praise him.

First, note again the 'fl' constructions: 'Fresh-firecoal chestnut-falls'; 'fold, fallow'; 'fickle, freckled'; and 'swift, slow'. They don't just describe the beauty they so admire, they attempt to embody it, with the 'f' and the 'l' running over each other like warp and weft to produce a contrasting texture of darkness and light. That which comes together by chance, the pied and the dappled, all those epiphenomena of the 'fl' force in Hopkins, do so as if artlessly, while nevertheless producing a beguiling beauty. They create the illusion of great artistry, perhaps, but were it planned, any such artistry would look merely artful. There is a beauty in chance, because chance makes these pied effects possible.

This 'fl' type of beauty which brings together chance, the divine, and the phenomenal, thereby reconfigures the 'argument by design' according to which God's benign existence may be inferred from the order in nature. In Hopkins such 'order' involves a degree of chaos, as in the Heraclitean epigram that 'the fairest order in the world is a heap of random sweepings'.[12] If God can be praised for dappled things, and if those things provide some manifestation of Him, then God must be associated with chance, disorder and the random effects of beauty they sporadically produce. One can always object that such 'randomness' is phony, having been designed by God, just as He ordered the chaos, but that would be to miss the point. It is rather that God, instead of having designed the world to a T, smiles on the randomness, the pied 'fl' effect, that His orderly world enables – as if there were, astonishingly, a degree of free will in nature, not just in man, a free will that is the opportunity for her to express herself in ways not preordained. Again one might object that it is only God who sanctions this freedom of the will in nature: but even if that's the case, He is not micro-managing it. The pied 'fl' effect represents the deft withdrawal, at least to a strategic point, of His designing hand, and this is what allows Hopkins to see nature not just as divine but as aesthetic in its own right. He is thanking God *for* dappled things, not ascribing divinity to them. God fathers-forth, but then lets them go; the 'forth' part of 'fathers-forth' signifies a sending away, a dispatching. Which means that 'manifestation' might be the wrong word, and my earlier remarks on God being reflected in nature can now be made more exact. Pied beauty, of which the 'fl' construct is an example, can and probably ought to be traced back to God, but it works as pied beauty only when that source is to some degree suppressed, concealed or left behind. When Hopkins writes, say, 'Fresh-firecoal chestnut-falls', there is a clear tension between the 'f's and the 'l's that alludes to divine energy, but at the same time they derive their own energy from taking the risk of surviving at a remove from the divine, by not acknowledging that origin and instead busying themselves only with their own internal combustion. The 'fl' effect is nothing less than the dimension of aesthetics defined as a space left alone by divine interference in order that it may stumble upon its own lovely, or at least compelling, random expressions. Too much God is bad for art, and if Hopkins is prone to interrogating his own religious faith, it is partly because it is this latitude from God that facilitates better poetry – poetry considered as the disclosure of pied beauty in all its awesome randomness. Faith in God and faith in language don't just complement each other, they also compete.

I believe this is one reason why Hopkins opts for 'inscape' rather than, say, 'being' or 'essence', both of which can be hard to wrest away from their origins in theological thought. There is a certain receding into its own horizons suggested by the entity that is blessed with inscape, which again speaks to a distance from, rather than a proximity to, God. That doesn't make inscape ungodly, far from it, but it does allow it greater freedom of individuation, and gives it permission to take upon itself its own unique markings (like 'fl'). It is a freedom to be singular, i.e. not part of an order, i.e. random; and because random, beautiful.

Up to a point, this concept of the aesthetic chimes with that of Kant's 'pulchritudo vaga' or 'free beauty'.[13] Kant wants to protect beauty from spoliation by human self-interest, by anything that could appeal to merely subjective emotion. He is suspicious, for example, of things that are 'charming' because charm works upon vanity: beauty that charms should probably not be taken as beautiful at all. Perhaps 'free beauty' could be used to describe the 'fl' effect in Hopkins, in its ability to present the beauty in nature and elsewhere without it serving a particular purpose, that of either God or human. It is a kind of beauty for beauty's sake, which would fit with the role of chance in it. Being chance, it has no purpose to fulfil, no agenda to pursue, such that when linguistic collisions like those between the 'f' and the 'l' occur, we the reader are supposed to be witnessing a movement seemingly without motive, effect seemingly without cause. Despite the fact that Hopkins' poetry is so heavily contrived that at one level it's hard to credit the notion of anything 'just happening' in his verse, that is how the 'fl' concept works, as unmotivated, stochastic beauty, free to associate where it will. Not that Hopkins wishes to document an infinite variety. Like earth's distance from the sun, the poetic distance from God creates benign conditions for all manner of creations to spawn, but, just as his poetry is so contrived, so the range of what Hopkins records is strictly limited. Or rather, his lexicon is so tightly defined, repetitious and idiomatic that the universe he reflects is correspondingly narrow; even at the level of an individual line like 'Fresh-firecoal chestnut-falls; finches' wings', the range of letters is strictly limited. He is a poet, not a natural scientist – free beauty only belongs to what he chooses to record.

It is part of what I would call his active passivity. On the one hand, Hopkins writes this surging, innovative, vigorous verse that jams itself right up under the skin of things, and quite on its own terms; on the other hand, he makes himself the servant of everything around him, almost to the point of abjection, even masochism – a passivity, in any case, that goes hand in hand with the freedom of nature, because it is a form of waiting for those striking permutations of matter to emerge. These contrary forces of the active and passive bind to one another like the 'fl' effect. For its part, the 'fl' effect too moves in these contrary directions, pretending on the one hand to mark the freedom of combination, as giving itself up passively to nature, while on the other hand working as a highly distinctive mark of Hopkins' own style, thus belonging entirely to the poet and actively asserting his mastery of a given poem.

In all cases, what Hopkins seeks is an *imprint*. Nature is heavily imprinted, just as the poetry is heavily imprinted – there are no light touches, nothing impressionistic – and he is attracted to the combination of 'f' and 'l' letters not only because they are effectively his sigil, they are almost literally a rubber stamp – when placed close to each other, they form a rubbery solidity that can still bend – that demonstrates perfect stamping. They show how the world should be stamped poetically upon paper, as nature has been stamped with pied effects. Yes, the words in Hopkins are so annealed that they seem like things, but they seem like things more because the sense of their having been pressed upon the page is so strong, and with a pressure that can come only from something that has substance. No doubt Hopkins might wish that words had such substance, but what is preferable is that they leave the physical impression that substantial things leave. The 'fl' effect, in other words, points to the receiving matter. Not just the page either, but the poet himself, and even his 'flesh', one of the most common words in Hopkins, and the longest entry in the four entire pages of 'fl' words listed in the Hopkins concordance. As I was saying in relation to the use of the word 'flesh' in 'That Nature is Heraclitean Fire', the flesh is for sure the sign of mortality, and the stretching of its muscles done by the 'fl' at the beginning only exposes it to a more imminent death: but the flesh is also a surface for receiving marks, most pointedly represented by the stigmata on Christ's body, the ultimate imprint.

I would like to finish by looking at one of the famous sonnets. It opens with a classic 'fl' construct:

> I wake and feel the fell of dark, not day.
> What hours, O what black hours we have spent
> This night! what sights you, heart, saw; ways you went!
> And more must, in yet longer light's delay.[14]

The light of day gets deferred until the end of the line, and after a late caesura. So Hopkins wakes into the anti-morning of reverse time, a creature born into uncreatedness. This is the time before light has been made, thus where no proofs of God, certainly not by design, are available. The creatureliness is borne out by the 'fell', the animal skin furnishing the primitive scene with an ambivalent comfort: a comfort blanket and a horrific dewlap of animal. He is as if waking in a cave. The seriousness of the threat to faith is there in the language. In the 'f' and 'l' words, 'feel the fell', the 'l's have been pushed apart from the 'f's, attenuating and enervating the energy, decreasing the stress in their labial play, and so, because decreasing the stress, also thinning out the divinity. The flashes and flecks of the Godhead are subdued to a more querulous and drawn-out, insinuating, searching and doubting combination: 'feel the fell'. There is no vision in those vowels; they are as blind as a worm. The horizontality of 'feel', that of the gropingly wakened supine sleeper, has nothing to drop into it from the vertical and relieve it. What falls, ironically, is only falling itself; the 'fell', the completed and perhaps irredeemable condition of creatureliness. The fell is also a dull chime ringing the distant counter-rhythm of night-time, associating all too easily with the fell of what is felled (like the poplars at Binsey); a death-knell too. A death-knell because, as is borne out in the second stanza, hours become life, where life is a euphemism for death, like a prison sentence. The creature's sacrifice is announced, and the fell is the skin that will be culled from the dead animal; as if Hopkins' body has been thrown into the slaughter truck with other poisoned beasts, and he wakes to this grim knowledge – 'fell' can also mean 'evil'. The evil commands the sense of error, the ways travelled by the heart in the underworld, the need to correct hours by years, then life (words which reinforce the sense of incarceration). The error is compounded in that his is a false sacrifice because he is poisoned. It is slaughter, not sacrifice; and his entire existence a gross, unfit parody of the martyr or witness. He becomes the very adulteration of the Eucharist in the last two stanzas, poisoned wine and 'dull dough'.

> With witness I speak this. But where I say
> Hours I mean years, mean life. And my lament
> Is cries countless, cries like dead letters sent
> To dearest him that lives alas! away.
>
> I am gall, I am heartburn. God's most deep decree
> Bitter would have me taste; my taste was me;
> Bones built in me, flesh filled, blood brimmed the curse.
>
> Selfyeast of spirit a dull dough sours. I see
> The lost are like this, and their scourge to be
> As I am mine, their sweating selves; but worse.[15]

There is a conventional contrast between spirit and letter, Hopkins being an agent of 'dead letters', and a 'dull dough' unleavened by the yeast that is the Holy Ghost ('yeast' and 'ghost' belonging to the same semantic family). But the dead letters also exacerbate the erroneousness of misdirected prayer; the prayer can always go astray, and God remain unenlightened as to our individual darkness. The prisoner's letter fails to reach the powers that be. The human letters are contrasted in turn with the letter of the law, the decree and anathema that can pour down brimstone for those in whom 'blood brimmed the curse'. It is in awe of such punishment that the latent sexual imagery of his sweating self flits.

Despite the tendency toward ignominious slaughter rather than the sacrifice of the martyr, there is a hint of religious longing for glory, and a complex identification with Christ. The autophagous zeal, the self-cannibalizing fervour of the third stanza, could almost be attributed to a kind of 'My God, why hast thou forsaken me?', where the suffering will end in the unbinding and redistribution of the flesh and blood of the body. So the verse risks speaking in the place of Christ. The binding and unbinding of Christ's body is the most divine stress of all.

This poem has been slowed down to a viscous ineluctability quite at odds with the flight-filled swooping randomness of the Christ-bird in 'The Windhover'. Sickly claustrophobia impedes the openness to being traversed by lines of flecked light: there is not even the flecked light coming through the prison bars. The Lethean 'sights' seen with the nightmarish eye are a far cry from the inner vision of faith; the sights are epic, pre-Christian, atavistic. 'Life' has this very quality, the quality of life before life, that is, before the life of Christ. Life in an animalistic age before faith, reversed through time where even the word 'life' destroys the energy of the 'f' and 'l' combination by inverting them. Or at the very best it is life before the New Testament, hence the Old Testament idiom of lamentation. Perhaps that is why the testamentary 'witness' is so isolated, a constituency of one lacking external corroboration; and why the lines

> And my lament
> Is cries countless, cries like dead letters sent
> To dearest him that lives alas! away.

recall the voice of John the Baptist calling hoarse in the wilderness, going his 'ways' like a mad evangelist, announcing the coming of Christ, but desperately uncertain as to his appearing. The dead letters raise the dreadful prospect of an uncompleted typology. Worse, they suggest the literal literality of scripture, mere words unstressed, as here the syntax lapses into the poetic orthodoxy of simile: 'cries like dead letters sent'.

The poem is a staggering through Hopkins' conscience, a conscience made so queasy by the knowledge that he is playing a dangerous game. Again it is a question of faith in language – there is so much faith in language, so much obsession with the 'fl' construct and what it stands for as a poetics, that his religious faith, as expressed in language – his 'faith, in language' – gets compromised. The withdrawal of God can go too far and suck too much light out of the world, leaving the poetry both richer and more desperate.

9

Symons in the decade of decadence

Pastel: Masks and Faces

The light of our cigarettes
Went and came in the gloom:
It was dark in the little room.

Dark, and then, in the dark,
Sudden, a flash, a glow,
And a hand and ring I know.

And then, through the dark, a flush
Ruddy and vague, the grace
(A rose!) of her lyric face.[1]

One could begin an analysis of Symons' poem in fairly conventional terms. Notice, for example, the rhythm of redoubled undulation, as the poem swells in the second stanza, holds itself in 'And a hand and ring I know', then bodies itself forward again with another flush, in a wavelike crescendo hinted at in one of the poem's quasi-French words, 'vague', French for 'wave'. The intensification has visual form in the darkening from orange to red, from the phosphorous light of cigarettes to the ruddy face. The ascent from hand of cigarette and ring, to the face, finds reinforcement in the words 'A rose' that sound out 'arose'. And so on.

But there are plenty of reasons for not dwelling on this poem, not least its sub-optimal tradecraft. The word 'Sudden' in line 5 is made redundant by 'a flash' coming after it: is any flash not sudden? Besides, 'sudden', like 'suddenly', is probably the most naive way conceivable of expressing narrative drama. If you must use it, use it like Eliot uses it, say, in 'Burnt Norton':[2]

> The detail of the pattern is movement,
> As in the figure of the ten stairs.
> Desire itself is movement
> Not in itself desirable;
> Love is itself unmoving,
> Only the cause and end of movement,
> Timeless, and undesiring
> Except in the aspect of time
> Caught in the form of limitation
> Between un-being and being.
> Sudden in a shaft of sunlight
> Even while the dust moves
> There rises the hidden laughter
> Of children in the foliage
> Quick now, here, now, always—
> Ridiculous the waste sad time
> Stretching before and after.

Eliot's 'sudden' is as bracing as the dive into a cold river. Coming after the wizened Aristotelianism before it, it pushes us back from the philosophy and launches us forthwith into the sensuous reality of the fresh, if sepia-washed, giggling of children. The contrast is huge, and the 'sudden' merited. The change of gear winds us, whereas in the Symons the juxtaposition of dark and light is just too obvious, too studied:

> Dark, and then, in the dark,
> Sudden, a flash, a glow,

The impact of the sudden flash has also been prefigured, and to that extent undermined, by the light of the cigarettes in the first line.

Besides, the repeated 'dark' doesn't fit with the 'gloom' in the first stanza – gloom you can still just about see in, but this heavy 'dark' you cannot; and in any case 'gloom' belongs more to the outside than the interior of a room. But worse is Symons' deployment twice of 'and then'. It is the crudest narrative device known to man, not to mention how awkwardly the second instance of it only adds to the already maladroit pile of 'and's in the previous line, 'And a hand and ring I know'; nor the odd character that 'and' takes on in the peculiar phrase, 'went and came', which is back to front.

The words 'sudden' and 'and' in this poem tell the tale of a poet with no idea about telling a tale, no narrative flair, but this incapacity on Symons' part can be redescribed in his favour. For what is Symons trying to do? He is trying to paint a picture, a 'pastel'. Like the true poet, the one who, on my definition, inclines towards the image, he wants to capture a moment as it stands out from the sequence of cause and effect that may have led up to it. If he uses 'sudden' and 'and then', it is because these are the shortest, least intrusive means of constructing a background against which that image – the light of cigarettes in the dark, the face sashaying from behind – can come alive. For Symons, narrative is ground, not figure. Actually it is the ground that serves figure, hence the ostensibly primitive line 'It was dark in that little room', which doesn't know if it is poetry or prose, but which hopes the darkness of the little room will impress itself better upon us if situated in the obvious narrative time of 'It was'. If Symons uses narrative devices such as 'sudden', 'and then' and 'it was', it is in a pedagogical spirit: clunky as they are, they are there as teaching devices to help us see what he wants us to see – the image.

For all that, there is only so much this base narrative ground can do to abet the image's coming to light, because the image itself, like a Platonic photocopy, is dog-eared on arrival. In Symons' poem, we find ourselves in a complex fantasy in which the image of masks and faces is itself hidden behind layers of masking. Which isn't necessarily a bad thing, because the atmosphere Symons wants to evoke in his pastel is that of a largely pleasant, if slightly menacing, confusion based on not quite knowing where something has come from. These layers begin well back in the literary canon, starting with masks and masking, so classic a topic for literature, with its origins in Greek drama and Greek drama's overlap with religious and pre-religious ritual. To choose them as a theme in a

nineteenth-century lyric is a belated, even hackneyed gesture, but
again that is part of the point, for the genealogy of the concept of
masking gives the poem a deep-sunk anchor while revealing next
to nothing about that genealogy – there is real value bestowed on
the word 'vague'. The brittleness of the Greek mask then balances
against the plasticity of faces, thus setting up the wider opposition
in the poem between stylized, formal procession and a feline,
dance-like suppleness. The phrase 'masks and faces' in the title
invites us to picture the mask put aside from the face, then covering
it again, and so on in a sort of magician's trick, while we marvel
at the textural difference between flesh and clay. So the mask is
layered not only in the sense that it tacitly refers back to the mask
in literary tradition, but also because it makes a layer over the face;
in both cases the top layer hides the layer beneath while also letting
us know it is there.

Other layers lie in between, all smudging each other, many taken
from a Frenchified aesthetic exemplified by Manet (particularly the
'Olympia'), Degas, Toulouse-Lautrec, and Baudelaire's own 'Le
Masque':[3]

Approchons, et tournons autour de sa beauté.
Ô blasphème de l'art! ô surprise fatale!
La femme au corps divin, promettant le bonheur,
Par le haut se termine en monstre bicéphale!
— Mais non! ce n'est qu'un masque, un décor suborneur,

I quote these particular lines mainly for their tone, in which I hear
the docent guiding us through an exhibition – the poem is about
a sculpture – which Symons seems to have hoped to emulate. For
example, Symons' last verse:

And then, through the dark, a flush
Ruddy and vague, the grace
(A rose!) of her lyric face

can be heard as lines spoken by a cultured if pretentious guide,
so that the title 'Pastel: Masks and Faces' can be heard in turn to
signal that it is a poem *about* a pastel, an ekphrasis, rather than
a metaphorical pastel of its own. Behind the elegant stupefaction,
there is explanatory intent, even though Baudelaire's poem takes us

far beyond explanation toward a gothic horror – that of the mask peeled away from the face – of which there is only the faintest residue in Symons whose constitution appears comparatively delicate. Few, in any case, would disagree that Symons' verse is a kind of copy of Baudelaire's or that, because he is so derivative, he belongs in a lower poetic league than the Frenchman; and to argue that his copy of Baudelaire has been deliberately faded to produce a more shabby chic effect would be too clever.

But there are other ways of understanding Symons' endemic secondariness. Though it is written in English, 'Pastel: Masks and Faces' is no English poem – culturally speaking. The English is stilted enough to sound like a translation, for a start, but more importantly its wardrobe of props comes from a Continental, and specifically Parisian setting. Symons is effectively importing delicacies from abroad, like a grocer's merchant who has had his head turned by the glamour to be found in Montmartre. But because English poetry had (and has) for so long been so largely averse to foreign influences – it is less a lie than mere exaggeration to say that from Symons you have to jump all the way back to Chaucer and the court of Richard II to find genuine openness in English poetry to French fancy – he will only ever find a niche market for his poetic products back in his homeland. His prose, on the other hand – the seminal 'Symbolist Movement in Literature'[4] – exerted genuine influence, as is well known, on such leading lights as Eliot and Yeats, who followed the trail to Verlaine, Laforgue, Rimbaud and so on. The book of prose made a bridge across the Channel, on which he tried to hawk his poetry, that is, own-brand imitations alongside the real thing: imitations in which the British origins are, however, masked only so far, for one can choose to hear the heavy-handed narrative devices that I've noted – 'and then', 'it was' – not as bad narrative, but good empiricism in the Anglophone tradition. These narrative inserts simply state the case. Whence another layer, Symons fitting the mask of the *flâneur* over a Cornish/Welsh identity.

In other words, the poem is as much a commendable attempt at yoking together two divergent poetic traditions, British and French, as a failure in reproducing the style of the latter. That is not the only dichotomy Symons is trying to resolve. As I mentioned, the poem is both a pastel and about a pastel, both a literary and an artistic work. No, it's not *literally* a pastel, nor could it be, but it does everything it can because it wants to say that the layered imagery it depicts is layered *imagery*, food first for the eyes – closely followed by the other senses – in relation to which the words of the poem are themselves to be understood as being as transparent, as little mask-like, as can be. Again we can reinterpret the narrative devices such as 'and then', which become empirical to the point of self-effacement; that ostensibly dull line, 'It was dark in the little room' is a way of minimizing incursion by words. Although there is the slightest hint of children's storybook whimsy in the lines, a nostalgia for seeing and hearing simple, delightful words on the page, on the whole the language seeks to get out of the way, to be even less than narrative ground, to swallow itself up so that all we have is the picture hanging before our eyes, with everything else blacked out, as if peering at it from under the hood of a camera. Given the choice, the poem would rather be picture than poem, especially as that Parisian setting, with its flushes and blushes, seems to call more for painting than writing. The only restraining force on this urge is that the sensibility behind the poem is, and wants to remain, poetic. Although equally bohemian, the figure of the poet, more than that of the painter, carries the almost imperceptibly superior intellectual refinement, as well as a soupçon of academic prestige, two attributes which this poem would like us, the reader, to subliminally acknowledge.

This tension between poetry and painting makes it hard to define the poem's genre. Is it a lyric? And is 'lyric' a genre or a catch-all for short poems of a generally appealing demeanour? An English 'lyric' tends to understand itself as part of a bloodline going back via Spenser, among others, to Virgil, a line that proceeds onwards to, say, Housman and other destinations very different from nineteenth-century Paris. Unless, that is, you consider 'lyric' a form of entertainment, the strumming of the lyre in front of a leisured audience, in which case it smacks of a decadence fitting for Symons' poem. What can we infer from Symons' use of it in 'her lyric face'? Does the entertainment aspect of lyric refer in this case to the music hall, and with it the larger scene we imagine beyond this dark room, where there is illicit revelry and private trysting? It is another strange phrase, and again perhaps because it sounds like a bad translation. What is a lyric face? For all the rapture provoked in his pastel by imagery, this lyric face is very hard to picture. The 'grace' that rhymes with 'face' perhaps indicates nobility, even the statuesque, which would make the lyric of the lyric face somewhat classical after all. If so, then the apposition of 'lyric' and 'face' echoes the larger apposition of hardness and softness, coldness and warmth. That would just leave the rose to be accounted for – and what could be more fitting for a lyric than this iconic flower?

Because the rose points at once to sexual experience and sexual innocence, however, it functions equally as an icon of the poem's own hesitant eroticism, which leads us to another set of polarities. The speaker could well be a lover, rising to seize the 'hand and ring I know', but the same line contains as much deference as sexual possessiveness. The phrase belongs to a little boy reaching for his mama, but also to the philanderer all too accustomed to buying rings for mistresses, inspecting his latest purchase. The entire last stanza

> And then, through the dark, a flush
> Ruddy and vague, the grace
> (A rose!) of her lyric face.

may be a discreet way of describing the woman's orgasm; at the same time it is a harmless piece of melodrama, in which the only effect is aesthetic. The dark room is likely the rendezvous used for the relief of sexual tension in the arms of a stranger, or at least arranging it, yet the 'little' makes it sound homely, like a parlour.

Actually, the room is more than ambiguous. Preceded by, for instance, John Donne ('We'll build in sonnets pretty rooms'),[5] Symons wouldn't be the first poet to allow a connection between a room mentioned in a poem and the poem itself as a room for the scene witnessed inside it (with those first two lines, 'Went and came in the gloom:/ It was dark in the little room', Symons is also succeeded by Eliot's 'In the room the women come and go' from 'Prufrock').[6] The room is the poem, the poem the room, and what matters is their boundedness, the contained space allowing for controlled effects that can operate in close concert. By keeping extraneous matter out, the room-poem – and perhaps this applies to lyric more generally – can focus on the matter proper to it, on that which has a right of access based on affinity with elements already within. Like the gallery space in Baudelaire's 'Le Masque', the room collects a carefully curated series of images, and rejects others. It is the place of Symons' personalized repertoire, the

artefacts that make up the limited, specialist inventory from which
he repeatedly draws them. Here, for example, are the first two of
the three stanzas of 'Impression':

> The pink and black of silk and lace,
> Flushed in the rosy-golden glow
> Of lamplight on her lifted face;
> Powder and wig, and pink and lace,
>
> And those pathetic eyes of hers;
> But all the London footlights know
> The little plaintive smile that stirs
> The shadow in those eyes of hers.[7]

It's not just that 'Impression' and 'Pastel: Masks and Faces' are
practically versions of each other, it's that their linguistic furniture,
so to speak, comes from the same room mentioned in the latter
poem, this room being more than mere setting for the scene with
the lady, and more even than the poem's metaphor of itself. What
it is, effectively, is Symons' archive. Through the dark in the poem
the speaker is seeing as much the inert contents of this archive as
a live encounter. Each individual poem is contained like a room,
but because the containment serves to keep foreign material out
and familiar material in, it happens that each individual poem has
only such familiar items to turn to, with the result that each shares
them with other poems, as if there were connecting doors between;
or as if, rather, there were a single originary room, still as small as
either, where all the stock is kept. I hesitate to label this room the
psyche of the poet, because it doesn't necessarily exist outside the
poems themselves. Nor, despite my choice of the word 'originary',
is it a trove of Platonic forms, where the essence, say, of Rosy
Glow is stored, leaving the poems themselves to make do with
watered-down versions.

So if have spoken about copying effects in Symons, I should
now be more precise. Yes, Arthur Symons arrives at the end of a
long tradition of literature concerned with masks, which inevitably
renders his own poem a kind of copy, let alone the larger argument
to be had about literature as imitation of nature. Yes, this copy's
fadedness is nevertheless embraced for its decadent value, just as
the artificiality of the fin-de-siècle scene gives off a certain chic.

And yes, the play of copies makes the poem an illusionist's trick, a devilishly foreign connivance, despite a residual decorum that stems, conceivably, from the poet's non-Continental upbringing. But we also have a weirder effect going on, whereby the poem is, in short, a copy of itself. This effect applies to all 'strong' poets, as Harold Bloom would dub them: in so far as Symons pulls it off, he is not so secondary after all. It relates to what I was saying about the lexicon of Dylan Thomas in the chapter on rhetoric. With notable frequency, Symons' poems draw on a repertory of images so defined that they 'copy' each other. And yet the copy lacks an original, despite antecedents in Baudelaire: not, then, because Baudelaire didn't employ similar images, but because the precise selection of imagery by Symons, what it includes and excludes – what has keys to the room – is unique. The images are 'originary' with Symons, as opposed to being copies of an original belonging to Baudelaire or Aeschylus. When deployed in a poem, they have a certain depth, like that created by the backing of a pastel, acquired from their identity with the same image deployed in another.

As if to disown the fixedness, even the obsessiveness, in returning to the same set of images, 'Pastel: Masks and Faces' passes itself off as something altogether more lax. The room is a given, it seems, but within it there is movement. Three specific movements, in fact: 1) the coming and going of the light of cigarettes; 2) the hand and ring appearing with a flash; 3) the rising in a flush of her lyric face. These are intended to create a sense of refined, metropolitan theatricality, and easy intercourse. But the movement is a deception. First because of the brute fact that poetry, like painting, is not a temporal art, so these are not moving images but images of moving. Moving light, moreover: each of the three movements captures a lighting effect: cigarette light, the flash of the hand, the flush of the rising face. If it were a pastel, these would be three patches of coloured brightness, each differing from the other but taken from the same palette of orange, red and white, on a dark background. And (second point) it is the cigarette's *light*, the hand and ring's *flash*, the face's *flush*, that provide the grammatical centre of each phrase, meaning that it is the light per se that is the true subject; the hand, the face, the cigarette serve as its vehicles, rather than the other way around. In this sense, the poem takes a pace away from the figurative and towards the abstract. In so doing, it performs a semi-effacement of the figure, a semi-effacement of the face, if you like, as if the face, main mimic organ of the body, were becoming a mask. Hence 'masks and faces': if there is movement in the poem, it is in the imaginary transition between these two. Symons' writing of the light, his photo-graph, is over-exposed, the light dominating the face as to nearly white it out, nearly mask it, thanks to too much flash. The 'nearly' is crucial. The mask threatens but never quite manages to cover everything, so the life never quite freezes into death, though other images in the poem usher it to the brink: the little room's coffined darkness, the ash of cigarettes, the craving for grace, even the parody of last rites with a grasping of the ringed hand of the priest at the bedside, the Styx-like transit 'through the dark', the social underworld connoting the death to which it might lead – the hell, more to the point, as the poem is all too aware of the sinfulness it might be perceived as celebrating. But the lyric face, which could be that of Persephone, swimming up out of the darkness, bursts in at the eleventh hour to save it.

And just as the mask fails to harden completely into death, so the face fails to become a complete being. The face is only a synecdoche for the whole person, where synecdoche is so much the poem's chief trope that 'Pastel: Masks and Faces' reads like an exemplum from a rhetorician's handbook:

> The light of our cigarettes
> Went and came in the gloom:
> It was dark in the little room.
>
> Dark, and then, in the dark,
> Sudden, a flash, a glow,
> And a hand and ring I know.
>
> And then, through the dark, a flush
> Ruddy and vague, the grace
> (A rose!) of her lyric face.

The face is a synecdoche for the body, and is preceded by the flush that is a synecdoche for the face. That is one 'nest'. The phrase 'hand and ring', in which a ring is a synecdoche for a hand, and a hand for a body, makes a second, more complex nest that also nests inside the first in so far as the 'hand and ring' combine as a synecdoche for the face and indeed the person whose face it

is. The hand also belongs to a third nest of synecdoches begun
by the cigarettes, which are synecdoches for the hands that hold
them. Arguably there is a fourth, if you count the light of the
cigarettes as a synecdoche for the flash it prefigures. The nesting
works like a Russian doll, going from smaller to larger (cigarette
to hand-and-ring to face to person), though with some siblings or
cousins complicating the otherwise straight-up-and-down sequence
of generations. Apart from the room which, as I have suggested,
is caught up in a nesting logic of its own, the only object in the
poem not to sit in one of these synecdochic nests is the rose which,
despite appearing to qualify 'grace', is probably nothing more
than a simile for the ruddy, vague, flushed face. Perhaps that's
why it is bracketed off, the exclamation mark asking forgiveness
for spoiling the series. Perhaps too it is why the exclamation '(A
rose!)' doesn't achieve the dramatic impact it shoots for – the
drama of the poem lies rather in the discoveries as each nest opens
into the next, and where the 'know' in 'hand and ring I know'
might signal not so much knowledge as the tantalizing promise of
its arrival – as in 'I know that hand and ring, but can't quite place
it'. The value of the synecdoche is not vested solely in the drama,
however. Synecdoche works not only by *alluding* to the larger piece
of the object of which it reveals the smaller, according to the 'pars
pro totis' formula, the part standing for the whole: in doing so, it
also *suppresses* the larger piece. The inked-in darkness of Symons'
pastel coincides with this suppressed area. In other words, the
darkness is more than darkness, it is active occlusion, this time
for epistemological rather than aesthetic purposes, that keep the
reader 'in the dark' as to what it masks. The poem adores its own
imagery, but its aesthetic preoccupations are forced to compete
with a drama of knowing and not-knowing. While synecdoche
concentrates the patches of light in the poem for aesthetic effect,
it also keeps us guessing, as it displays a comparable talent for
epistemological feint.

None of this implies that the hand, the face, the cigarettes
don't have a semiotics of their own. Especially 'cigarettes', which
perhaps because it is a French word with a feminine ending, recalls
artisanal words like 'moquette', 'palette', 'pirouette', and so evoke
again the bohemian atmosphere of the city that Walter Benjamin
named the capital of the nineteenth century. It is an atmosphere
the poem wants to trap in its room so Symons can savour it all the

more, though this misses the point. Between being bohemian and writing about bohemia there is a fine line that Symons sometimes crosses. The 'our' of 'our cigarettes' is too convivial, for example. He is a legitimate character in that modernity which stretches from Baudelaire (who is sometimes attributed with the first significant use of the word 'modernity') to Benjamin himself, but chiefly as an enthusiast. And we readers, like Symons, can easily give in to romanticizing that modernity along with its cigarettes, its cities, its poets, its *flâneurs*, its garrets, its music halls, its painted ladies. For that matter, one can easily give in to the opposite – deploring Symons and his kind for their bourgeois lifestyles, their degenerate leisure, and the degree to which aesthetic poetry such as this 'masks' the material truth about the industrializing cities where it is set. The figure of the prostitute which Symons often turns to, for example, a figure which 'Pastel: Masks and Faces' might concern, is treated as a fascinating subject for Symons' imagineering only to the extent that he glosses over the grim reality of the sex trade in nineteenth-century European cities.

Of course Symons' poem is determined by its cultural and political context, but not entirely. It is also absolutely singular, and it turns out to be an extraordinarily successful failure.

10

High Windows, reframed

When I see a couple of kids
And guess he's fucking her and she's
Taking pills or wearing a diaphragm,
I know this is paradise

Everyone old has dreamed of all their lives—
Bonds and gestures pushed to one side
Like an outdated combine harvester,
And everyone young going down the long slide

To happiness, endlessly. I wonder if
Anyone looked at me, forty years back,
And thought, *That'll be the life;*
No God any more, or sweating in the dark

About hell and that, or having to hide
What you think of the priest. He
And his lot will all go down the long slide
Like free bloody birds. And immediately

Rather than words comes the thought of high windows:
The sun-comprehending glass,
   And beyond it, the deep blue air, that shows
Nothing, and is nowhere, and is endless.[1]

Though completed in 1967, this poem lent its title to the 1974 Faber volume in which it was later collected, a fact that makes it the signature dish of that collection, the poem which the poet (or publisher, or both) considers the best or most representative example of the poetry he's lately penned. 'If you read only one poem from the collection, read this,' the title seems to advise. Unless, that is, cannibalizing the title of an individual poem for the collection as a whole points to a lack of imagination, as in: 'I can't think of anything better: *High Windows* will have to do for the whole thing.' Even so, the phrase 'High Windows' has been chosen over others. It may not be the killer title, but it is the least bad example.

So when we come to this poem, we are already in the land of examples, of cases in point, and the very first line, 'When I see a couple of kids' picks up the theme. 'When I see' stands for 'Whenever I see' (as opposed to 'At the point when I shall see'), implying that seeing a couple of kids happens with sufficient frequency for each couple to add to the examples of the phenomenon that 'I' am now about to identify. A few lines on we have

> I wonder if
> Anyone looked at me, forty years back,
> And thought, *That'll be the life*

which do a similar thing – 'I wonder if anyone thought of me back then as an example of the paradise to come'. He and his 'lot' are a batch, a sample that exemplifies a certain way of life to be both envied and deplored (in that order).

I'll come back to the individual lines, but first I want to explore this notion of exemplification, and particularly whether 'High Windows', the poem rather than the collection, if they can be separated, exemplifies anything at all. The point being that when we treat poems as examples of a general x, we are more likely to miss their specific y. Take again the opening lines:

> When I see a couple of kids
> And guess he's fucking her and she's
> Taking pills or wearing a diaphragm,

And now imagine a commentary on them that runs as follows:

These three lines don't just describe the scene they describe. They embody a theory of poetry, namely that poetic language needn't always be beautiful. It can even be ugly. Listen to their harshness, which after the lyric promise of the title 'High Windows' is especially astringent. There is an emetic splutter of 'k' consonants – 'couple', 'kids', 'fucking', 'Taking' – and even the 'g' in 'guess' verges on a 'k', toughening in turn the aspirated 'g' in 'diaphragm'. They announce with both excitement and defiance, that 'I am a poem proving the thesis that ugliness does not lie beyond poetry's remit. The doctrine of aesthetic beauty in poetry is probably no more than foppish affectation.'

This warts-and-all approach, which in its emphasis is ironically flamboyant, is the kite-mark of Movement poetry, which thinks of itself as plain-speaking in a plug-pulling and phlegmatically English kind of way. Movement poetry of the fifties and sixties had for a while a counterpart in the 'Kitchen Sink' art of roughly the same period. Both the art and the poetry are linked to a post-war tightening of economic belts in Britain, the carry-over of the ration-book mentality, and the mucking-in sharing-out of menial tasks. Lyric poetry of the post-Victorian variety is an unconscionable luxury unless revamped as a civic salve that articulates post-war melancholy and loss for the benefit of the man on the street. It is a period when the status of war victim and economic victim broadly merge, prompting sentiments of equality that take institutional form in Attlee's Welfare State.

That gritty realism leaves its stain on the first three lines of 'High Windows', which is an essay in miniature on social aspirations and their limits. That said, the poem, completed in 1967, is equally a response to the later sixties and hippy culture. Remember Larkin's quip that sexual intercourse began in 1963, 'rather late for me'. The poem might have its roots in post-war husbandry, but what it dramatizes is the encounter between the self-denying ordnances of that era and the permissive habits of the one that follows, the Swinging Sixties that provoke such bemusement and gall in those of Larkin's generation who were born too late to have experienced anything like it say at the height of the British empire, and too early to now pluck the swinging fruits. They have missed out at both ends. The accident

of their birth was much less subject to control, so the 'birth
control' figured in the pills and the diaphragm is all the more
nettling.

It is a commentary that treats 'High Windows' as a document of
its time, an 'example' of the Zeitgeist, or at least a response to it.
Which may be true. I am not saying this is not a poem about a
middle-aged man (a.k.a. Philip Larkin) overtaken by a socio-sexual
revolution that has left him on the hard shoulder, but that such a
reading is obliged to gloss over peculiarities in the phrasing that sit
with it most awkwardly. Namely the following:

1   Lines 2 and 3 define the couple as boyfriend and girlfriend,
    but the phrase 'couple of kids' in line 1 had indicated
    a couple as in 'two individuals, not sexually connected,
    momentarily going along together', leaving the reader the
    task the poem itself has ducked, of reconciling conflicting
    images of the same object. Or is Larkin playing a trick
    on us, whereby the first line lulls us into a false sense
    of security, in which we believe we are getting a poem
    about two children, only for that illusion to be shattered,
    shockingly, with the adult language of 'fucking' that is such
    a stark counterpoint to the 'kids' we momentarily thought
    they might have been? Maybe.

2   The longer phrase of which 'couple of kids' is a component,
    'When I see a couple of kids and guess' doesn't sound right.
    It is hard to imagine anyone using such a construction in
    the ordinary speech that the poem, based on its opening
    line, wants to affect: 'When I see a couple of kids and
    think', perhaps, but not 'guess'.

3   'Taking pills' should be 'taking the Pill' if it isn't to suggest
    the girl has a nameless affliction, leading the poem off on
    an altogether different tack.

4   The brutalist language sounds less than 100 per cent
    owned by the speaker of it. From certain angles one can
    detect otherwise invisible quotation marks around 'kids'
    and 'fucking'. Is he mocking the language used by the
    kids? If so, we have an example (the language used by the
    couple of kids) within an example (the couple of kids as

an example of a wider social phenomenon), but it is not clear. Is he, rather, trying the words on in order to extract a vicarious thrill? The first three lines shoot their mouth off with a vocabulary so contemporary as to be almost out of time with its time. Hippies would be too 'peaceful' to countenance it; and the cussing has been derived from the Angry Young Man era of the previous decade. The lines either over or under-shoot their target. Perhaps that is a skilful way of representing the figure speaking them, who is out of touch with the times, *de trop*. Perhaps not.

5 There are not enough prepositions or conjunctions in the first five lines to make them flow, and the resulting feel of over-condensed prose cannot quite be excused on the grounds of a poetical economy with words.

6 The poem has much more to it than its dyspeptic opening, of course, and in particular what happens at the close. If you continue down the route of the cultural commentary I began, you arrive in the last stanza at a dead end. True, there is recourse to the claim that the line 'Nothing, and is nowhere, and is endless' affirms the existence of the harsh realities on which the speaker has reflected, precisely by portraying a turn away from them. But it is an argument inadequate to the line's signal emptiness.

Taken together, these factors may or may not amount to a damning of the stanza as poorly constructed, but they do suggest we are not dealing with straightforward social commentary: the hermeneutic signals are too awry. It is like looking at certain paintings by Lucian Freud, in which the exaggerated realism can cause you to miss the fact that the feet don't quite make contact with the ground they are supposed to be standing on.

Given these questions and concerns, I don't propose to approach the poem either as example or critique. If there is a reference to a diaphragm or a combine harvester, these are better understood as projections contained within the poem-space than unmediated reflections of the real world. Which, I admit, only raises further questions and concerns. If not the world to which we thought it referred, what is it that organizes this so-called poem-space? What makes those projections hang together? The conventional answer would be Larkin's psychology, by which account 'High Windows' is the poet's subjective construction of the world around him rather than a description of the world itself. And again, that may be true; there is no final answer. One alternative lies in the concept of what I would call the 'hidden legend', the condensed phrase, saying, proverb or moral of which a given text is the more expansive translation. In the case of 'High Windows' the hidden legend seems to be 'the facts of life', i.e. both what 'kids' are told about sex as well as the defiant, despotic facticity of empirical data. Up to a point, Larkin's poem can be considered an excursus on this phrase, a phrase unnamed within it, though even under this rubric we shall again run into problems accounting for the last lines.

Among the most cardinal facts of life on which the poem turns is that of ageing and the generation gap it opens up. Slouching along on the other side of this gap to that of the buttoned-up misanthropist who speaks the poem's opening lines are the 'kids' who may therefore be infantile, but have taken in their stride such redoubtable innovations as the Pill and the diaphragm. This implies that the generation gap signifies not just difference in age, but difference in Age: the speaker (who from now on I'll call PL) and the kids co-exist in the same temporal moment while inhabiting different time zones – PL the past, the kids the future. They share the moment without sharing it, which in the light of the tragicomic statement, 'Man hands on misery to man', in Larkin's 'This be the Verse', makes for a noteworthy disjunction.[2] 'This be the Verse' stares out at an unbroken chain of error, of mistakes repeated down the generations. 'High Windows' envisions the opposite, with the next generation making a decisive break from the past.

The poem goes on, however, to reframe this disjunction in a wider perspective that makes it seem more in order than at first. PL says:

I wonder if
Anyone looked at me, forty years back,
And thought, *That'll be the life*

From the perspective of his own elders, PL was to have made a break from the past too, 40 years before, identical in form if not content to the breaking away done by the 'kids' of today. The reframing discloses a continuous line of discontinuities, with each generation breaking from the generation before it, in a seamless sequence of ruptures. But no sooner does this reframing occur than it gets subsumed under another frame in which, as we are to infer from the element of sourness in PL's tone, no such break was ever made by him. He failed yesterday in a way the kids have succeeded today. In *this* frame, the disjunction represented by the kids is restored, but without the notion of the 'seamless sequence of ruptures' quite being displaced, because although PL and his lot failed to make their own break with the past, the possibility of them doing so was there, at least in the minds of their Victorian elders. What the generation gap really signifies is not so much that the kids of today have more opportunities than those of PL's generation, but that they seize them.

The result is a poem that belongs, despite its 'modernity', to a classic category, that of *carpe diem*. It is a category that Larkin nevertheless interprets freely, by contrasting days seized (by the couple of kids) with days wasted (by PL and his lot), rather than employing the *carpe diem* in the service of the sanguine exhortation for which it was designed. Kids, being self-exhorting, have reached a level of suave self-management, breathtakingly, leaving their seniors looking hopelessly fumbling and as though simply having missed the point, still making a virtue out of an outmoded necessity. Meanwhile, in a self-fulfilling prophecy, PL and his lot's lassitude, along with an overdeveloped sense of propriety, prevent them from seeing a way out of their lassitude and overdeveloped sense of propriety. Time being a preoccupation in Larkin's poems, presenting itself typically as a challenge: will it be seized or will its default setting prevail, which is for it to simply drain away? The choice is Larkin's version of 'To be or not to be', a choice between the active and the passive, in which the opportunity to perceive a choice at all is massively biased towards those of an active disposition, i.e. not him. For him, it wasn't to be.

It wasn't to be, and the poem stages the false choice between fatalism and choice itself, even in the smallest words. Larkin's use of 'forty', for example, evokes the inevitabilities of middle-age, the fact that life doesn't begin but ends at 40, and distantly recalls the 40 days and nights of ineluctable biblical edict that stand as a counterpoint to 'paradise'. As for the theme of choice, we get a 'couple' of kids, suggesting ease and variety of coupling rather than mid-century monogamy; the girl is taking pills *or* wearing a diaphragm, for even in the birth-control market there is consumer choice. But the larger choice is still false, not only because you have to start as a chooser in order to choose choice, but also because the fatalism of PL hasn't simply been imposed. There has to have been a degree of collusion with 'fate' or the poem wouldn't carry its note of failure – for failure, like success, can transpire only in a world that allows for some human self-determinism. PL is no pure victim, and if he and his lot have lived under the sign of necessity it has not been without a modicum of collusion or pride or masochistic pleasure. After all, pleasure *was* their preference, a fact betrayed by their indulging in such negative forms of it; any envy in the poem would have been converted into judgement if it wasn't.

Hence the loaded use of 'paradise': the paradise that PL et al. both could (had they had more wit) and could not (because of the times in which they were born) have had; the paradise of which the kids are putting on such a nimble demonstration; the paradise that the atheistic PL a.k.a. Philip Larkin knows he has ruled himself out of anyway, but which doesn't stop him privately salivating over earthly versions of it; the paradise that is earthly for the kids who get all their jam today; the paradise that doesn't have to be confined to a dream such as dreamed by 'everyone old'; the 'paradise' that mocks the language of the travel agent (cf. 'Come to sunny Prestatyn!'); the paradise that is not, therefore, the antithesis of the earthy language of the first three lines it was set up to be, but a logical consequence of them ... Despite these many nuances clinging to the word 'paradise', it achieves some purity of effect. The insolent vaguenesses in the first three lines ('a couple of', 'guess', 'pills or'), made soggier with the apathy of the half rhyme ('she's'/'paradise'), resolve unexpectedly into 'I know this is paradise'. It is a trope of clarification that will be recast at the end in the image of high windows, and so prepares us for it.

Sadly, paradise doesn't last (of course not), despite the promising absence after it of a full stop, which conjures up the endlessness reprised in both 'endlessly' and 'Nothing, and is nowhere, and is endless'. Like a raised barrier, that absence is there only to permit the word 'paradise' to drive on into the second stanza where it meets 'Everyone old'. What a comedown – it is as if paradise has taken a wrong turn into an old people's home. I mentioned the paucity of prepositions and conjunctions, which gives the poem the feeling here and there of botched prose: in order to run on properly to 'Everyone old', the word 'paradise' needed the definite article ('I know this is the paradise everyone old has dreamed of'). The clarifying air of 'I know this is paradise' was a little spurious. Whether or not that is the poet's solecism, the effect is to give paradise with one hand, and with the other to take it away. For PL and everyone old this double gesture appears like a sorry contradiction, admonishing them that they can't have their cake and eat it. The kids, meanwhile, know no such contradictions, their ability to reconcile the irreconcilable, to switch from a win/lose to a win/win mentality represented in the hairpin turn that takes us from the first three lines into the fourth:

> When I see a couple of kids
> And guess he's fucking her and she's
> Taking pills or wearing a diaphragm,
> I know this is paradise

That fourth line goes for maximum contrast with what has preceded. Having set out the earthly roughness of fucking and pills and diaphragms, so abrasively real as to make us wince, we are told what it all means: not hell, as we were anticipating, but heaven. You thought it was a contradiction? You thought wrong – that's old-school logic. The whole point of kid-dom is that it can assimilate divergent phenomena, heaven and earth, with so little effort.

The poem continues:

> Bonds and gestures pushed to one side
> Like an outdated combine harvester,
> And everyone young going down the long slide

> To happiness, endlessly.

By 'Bonds' PL is referring to solid social bonds, and even to the economic bonds of a prudent nation, represented at the local level by your upstanding bank manager; but the main reference seems to be the marital bonds that, before the days of mass contraception, would tie you in to the girl you got into trouble. Similarly, the 'gestures' point to the doing away with all the palaver of courtship, the protocols of wooing that would have involved, tediously, the parents of the boy and girl in question: the breeziness of the 'couple of kids', by contrast, owes much to the fact they're not chaperoned. PL is indulging in a bit of social anthropology, turning over a thesis about a shift away from the family as the basic unit of society. In fact, it is as if 'society' has slipped beyond the anthropologist's reach altogether, because the bonds and the gestures have been put aside, leaving no symbols to decipher, no codes to break. As we have been instructed by the language of the first stanza, what you see is what you get.

With the simile of the 'outdated combine harvester', the poem plays its trump card. Coming in at line 7 of 16, it is almost exactly the middle of the poem, and very much its imaginative centre – the sort of phrase that gets a poet remembered, the equivalent of a George Best goal. Though again it's a bit off. The bonds and gestures that PL has just referenced come from a stiff-backed, upholstered, middle-class context where you have to mind your Ps and Qs – from a provincial interior, in any case, that sits at a considerable distance from the fields where you might come across a combine harvester. So if the bonds and gestures have been pushed aside like an outdated combine harvester, it is because the pushing aside of anything considered outdated can be likened to the pushing aside of the aforementioned machine, not because there is any similarity between it and those bonds and gestures. However, the image of the rusting contraption with the ridiculous name, made all the more ridiculous as the weeds grow up through its axles, is so striking that the fact the simile only half works scarcely detains us.

Besides, the harvester combines with other image streams in the poem. With the pills we have been introduced to the notion of technological advance, so the combine harvester evokes a corresponding decline in the manufacturing sector, along with an irreversible shift away from the country and towards the town. More distantly rumbles the Stalinistic idea of agricultural productivity as the cornfield-lined road to heaven on earth, by which the very English combine harvester contains a sub-image in the Soviet tractor of Five Year Plan vintage. The notion of planning in this Communist sense is put into apposition with that of planning a family, the word 'combine' evoking the notion of the 'Soviet' as 'collective', and then getting double-entendred back into that of communes, love-ins and the free sex that depends for its freedom on contraception. The harvester activates the dormant connection in that first stanza between agriculture and copulation, telling us that the earth needs to be reaped. But being so outdated, it only becomes a metaphor for PL's penis that, being out of sync with its time, can't oblige – it no longer does much 'fucking', and the earth remains unreaped. And not just because of PL's inadequacy. It is also the combined effect of pills and diaphragms – no seeds, no fruits, no harvest.

If I ventured the claim that poems are sometimes invisibly organized by a 'hidden legend', perhaps a better contender for this poem than 'the facts of life' is 'Et Non In Arcadia Ego': a thwarted arcadianism is marbled right through it. 'High Windows' may be classified as an (anti-) *carpe diem*, and its imagery of fucking and harvesting plays well into the notion of making hay while the sun shines, the rosebuds PL fails to gather – imagery that connects with pastoral (we also have the priest and his implied flock). Like *Piers Plowman*, the poem opens with a vision of merry folk taking their pleasure, but because PL can't share in it, the poem is forced elsewhere, making its pastoral as circumscribed as that *carpe diem*. Rather than plough its own furrow and thus compete with the satyrs who are the copulating kids, it essays, at the suggestion of a paradise, a half-successful ascent towards high windows – half-successful because the poem is so like a hot-air balloon on an English Sunday, that on lift-off only lifts so far.

Inevitably, everyone young is going in the opposite direction. They have reached the top of the slide and are now coming down, as if to emphasize just how earthly this paradise has become: its heights go down and down, and again PL has been wrong-footed. The phrase 'down the long slide' does two things: it crabbedly reproves the slippery slope of moral decline while with priest-like duplicity it enjoys the prospect. Miraculously, the young don't just stop at the earth like the meteoric career of the ill-fated combine harvester, the feeble English contribution to superpower technology that, like a crashed Apollo rocket, becomes a museum-piece fallen to earth: they keep falling. The 'endlessly' takes the bottom out of Sodom and Gomorrah, fire and brimstone, for free love is airy vacuousness, weightlessness of the moon age. While for PL paradise has a flip-side in divine retribution and diabolism (the first stanza gives off a whiff of sulphur from PL), for the young paradise just keeps on going, without meeting its contrary, in an

economic and sexual apotheosis that is not even atheism, being
neither doctrinal nor counter-doctrinal, neither decline nor incline
– just pure inclination. And so the incline of the italics that follow
suggests all those things by which PL's generation is hemmed in: the
closet, the priest's garb, confession, repression, pudeur, conscience-
wrestling, defecation, onanism, private writing, prayer, deception,
paranoia, adultery, domestic shames:

> And everyone young going down the long slide
>
> To happiness, endlessly. I wonder if
> Anyone looked at me, forty years back,
> And thought, *That'll be the life;*
> *No God any more, or sweating in the dark*
>
> *About hell and that, or having to hide*
> What you think of the priest. He
> And his lot will all go down the long slide
> Like free bloody birds.

The simultaneous descent-ascent of the young getting so high as
they slide like 'kids', is told in the equally off image of birds: birds
go up, not down. As well as 'dolly-birds' and the possibility of a
lurking, Larkin pun on the lark ascending, these anti-gravitational
birds connote, by their pseudo-heaviness, the other bird that PL
carries around his neck for having tried to spoil the fun and ruin
the auspices of happiness: the albatross, the freebird that, bloody,
enslaves the one who is the bad one of his 'lot', of bad fate,
the devilish one who has killed it. That fits with the 'deep blue
air' of the final stanza, which seems like a marine sky, sponged
of omens, a sky of departure spied out nautically by the 'glass'
('sun-comprehending' also has an antique nautical ring). Like the
mariner, Larkin has stopped us, the guest, on the threshold of a
scene of young coupling, and enthrals us to too self-pitying a vision.
   The floating play of gravity, which has a touch of hysteria, plays
semantically on the grave: not just in the sweating in the dark about
hell or the figure of the priest, but in the digging of the earth, and
the long Letheward slide to happiness. Endlessly down and down,
to oblivion. The fall to Lethe hints to us that the bird descends
not only from Coleridge's albatross but Keats' nightingale, and the

final stanza makes this more explicit by using 'rather than words' to echo Keats' 'rather than thoughts', in the words 'Oh for a life of sensations rather than thoughts':

> And immediately

> Rather than words comes the thought of high windows:
> The sun-comprehending glass,
> And beyond it, the deep blue air, that shows
> Nothing, and is nowhere, and is endless.

Keats preferred sensations to thoughts, but Larkin turns towards thoughts rather than words, steering a course hard by romanticism without disembarking. This post-Keatsian 'rather' helps to set up what could be called the 'clinamen' of the final stanza, its unexpected swerve away from the logic leading up to it – a double swerve, in fact. The poem could and perhaps should have ended in resignation, even tragedy. The day can't be seized, we have been overtaken by the kids, so let's give up, let's kill ourselves. Instead of this ending, however, the poem swerves towards what at first looks like the transcendent, even sublime romanticism of the deep blue air. But then it swerves away from this too, into 'nothing'. Perhaps that's rather Keatsian, after all, himself 'half in love with easeful death', and playing dangerously nihilistic games.

It's not the nothing of the suicide, however, and the first clue is the word 'immediately' that obviously means 'without mediation'. Without PL mediating it comes the thought – a thought being a form of mediation, a noumenal tool for processing the phenomenal – of high windows which, made of glass, create the illusion of immediacy or non-mediacy (one looks through glass, not at it), while at the same time providing a mediating frame. There is a binary switching that runs as follows:

> *immediately* – without mediation
> *the thought* – with mediation
> *windows* – with and without mediation
> *sun-comprehending* – with mediation
> *glass* – with and without mediation
> *deep blue air* – without mediation

shows – with mediation
Nothing, and is nowhere, and is endless – without mediation

The frame is repeatedly withdrawn and replaced, like an optician trying on lenses to test a patient's eyesight. The trope of high windows *is* transcendental but more in the philosophical than literary sense: the high windows, glass and sun all 'transcendental' in so far as they make apparent the conditions of appearance (not forgetting the glassiness of the mariner's 'glittering eye'). And, being made apparent themselves, these things that make appearance apparent and are so consumed by light as to barely be objects – windows, glass and sun – nevertheless assume a certain phenomenal weight. These 'things', if that's what they are, are more than no-thing, more than nothing, but only just. At the very least, they are things by which 'nothing' is mediated.

In subjective terms, this play of mediation is telling us that PL has the means with which to mediate the world but not to experience it. The closest he gets to palpable reality is air and light, nothing grounded. This is the fate of the poet, trapped in an observatory of mediations, and as if to remind us of it, PL uses his signature phrase, 'high windows', bang in the middle of the stanza. Remember, 'High Windows' is also the name of the poem as well as the collection, so even the signature itself is framed by at least two further frames that reflect it like glass, before it meets the reality lying on the other side of that collection (small wonder it's hard to bracket this poem with the supposedly objective verse of Movement poetry). By this stacking of frames, the poem can create the illusion of having a genesis of its own, its own signature, that acts as a kind of consolation for having no 'kids', with the 'sun' in 'sun-comprehending' serving as a pun on 'son'. There's the sun but no son, comprehension and mediation without an heir becoming apparent in this genealogy of appearances and copies. The nothing evokes this childlessness and the infinity of the death of the bachelor, that forms such an ironic parallel to the childlessness 'planned' by the kids with their contraceptive gizmos.

There is, incidentally, another signature that Larkin has left in these lines, which I'll mention in a brief digression before finishing. The phrase 'high windows' puts the letters 'w' and 'n' in close proximity. These letters, like 'f' and 'l' in Hopkins, seek each other out in Larkin's verse. There is the collection *The Whitsun Weddings* (and the poem of the same name within that collection), and in 'High Windows' there is the opening 'When I'; then 'wearing a'; 'Everyone'; 'everyone young'; 'I wonder if'; 'sweating'; 'what you think'; 'will all go down'; 'shows nothing'; 'is nowhere'. In the poem printed in the collection on the opposite page, 'Forgot What Did', we have a whole concatenating run:[3]

Stopping the diary
Was a stun to memory,
Was a blank starting,

One no longer cicatrized
By such words, such actions
As bleakened waking.

I wanted them over,
Hurried to burial
And looked back on

Like the wars and the winters
Missing behind the windows
Of an opaque childhood.

And the empty pages?
Should they ever be filled
Let it be with observed

Celestial recurrences,
The day the flowers come,
And when the birds go.

So Larkin as PL has signed himself into 'High Windows'. After all the endless going down the long slide, the high windows seem to represent a final look up towards the heavens. Yet even the windows mediate that look, and the look itself is the thought of a look rather than the look itself. It is loss in the style of gain.

11

The case of J. H. Prynne

Prynne's poetry gets treated as a case of difficulty, a case of the violation of the principles of poetry, a case of wilful obscurantism, a case of misunderstood genius, a case of a poet ahead of his time, and so on. For the record, I believe all those captions to be true. Except that treating Prynne as a 'case' of anything is tacitly conceding that we haven't yet got the measure of him – it is a form of resistance and a way of avoiding the poems. When something as irruptive and non-conformist as the poetry of Prynne arrives on the scene, we want to treat it as a 'case' because it helps to contain the anxiety that case provokes. The case is a cage. A case is also what you have to solve in a criminal investigation, using techniques of decryption – as in 'Sherlock Holmes and the case of J. H. Prynne'. So challenging is this case that only a sleuth of Holmes' stature could crack it.

I'm not saying there is a way out of this conundrum. Perhaps some of the aggression one suffers as a reader reading Prynne has even been designed to ensure we treat him as a special case, as if we were dealing with a colossal vanity. The fact this is the last chapter of my book no doubt plays into this dynamic. Like Vasari's *The Lives of the Artists*, with its progression towards Leonardo, Michelangelo and Raphael, my (obviously less seminal) book could seem to be implying that Prynne marks the crowning moment of modern poetry. Who knows? Maybe he does.

So are we to simply lay aside the ambiguities of Prynne's status, and get straight to the poetry? Here is the poem I would like to consider:[1]

A blow on the side of the mouth
    strike harder, it is important
  to be lyrical and joyous
    then again, another
  on the neck, how can this
be done so strongly without
  the highest fidelity, for there is
    no cry, hardly as to know
is to loosen, being not part of sense
  or by auscultation, taking the air
and the force crushes up, blow upon
  the windpipe, next at a rush for breath
for in the spine direct from the eyes
    holding back the parts
    of the soul by black thuds
  you know you do: had you not better
    with a metal spike the axis
of ah, attention, no liquid, frame clipped
  by lapse indrawn and hit
    in no time or at all there is
  exactly to the front of this
    on the paper hoop as a form
    goes on through.

According to a marvellously instructive essay by John Wilkinson on *Word Order*,[2] the collection from which this poem is taken, the references, allusions and sources relevant to that collection (including therefore the poem above), run to at least the following:

1 Prynne's other poetry
2 Prynne's prose
3 Wordsworth's 'The Solitary Reaper'
4 Wordsworth and Coleridge's *Lyrical Ballads*
5 Heidegger
6 Hölderlin
7 Charles Olson

8 The Dachau prisoners, Jura Soyfer and Herbert Zipper, who wrote the Dachaulied (Dachau Song) in 1938

9 Schelling

10 Eugenio Montale's poem, 'Tempi Di Bellosguardo'

11 Nazi reasoning

12 Social Darwinism

13 The Dolmetsch recorder

14 Albert Ayler, the recorder virtuoso

15 The German drinking-song, 'Wer soll das bezahlen'

16 Shakespeare's *Measure for Measure, As You Like It* and Prospero

17 A coalminers' song 'representing the historical traditions defeated by financial 'disciplines' in the UK miners' strike of 1984–85'

18 Christ's stigmata

19 Open-heart surgery

20 Monsanto, the pharmaceutical company

21 Tudor carols

22 Joseph of Arimathea

23 Sea shanties

24 *Sir Gawain and the Green Knight*

25 Seventeenth-century English Puritan sermons

26 Kant

27 Hannah Arendt

28 Paul Gaugin

29 The guidelines on cardiopulmonary resuscitation (CPR)

30 Guido Fackler's study on music in concentration camps

31 Douglas Oliver

32 Chaucer

33 Rilke

Despite the length of the list and the scholarly effort it must have cost him to assemble it, Wilkinson modestly calls his gloss 'partial'. And for sure, it's not the last word on the subject: further allusions will be turned up by other readers – and in a moment I'll venture a couple of my own.

I wish to take nothing away from Wilkinson's reading – it represents an invaluable resource – but I wonder whether, just as treating Prynne as a 'case' speaks to a certain anxiety, this marinading of Prynne's poetry in its sources signals an anxiety of its own. Although Wilkinson embraces Prynne to the point of here and there imitating the master's prose style and following some of his affectations (like preserving the diphthong in the word 'synæsthesia'), it too comes across as a defence against it, as if each reference unturned is another brick in the wall of robust reading. Might the adjective 'partial' be a tad disingenuous? Is there a bit of Wilkinson defying us to outscore him on his references?

Either way, after reading Wilkinson it is with an irreversible loss of readerly innocence that we go back to Prynne. Not that Wilkinson takes all the blame: other critics and Prynne himself appear to demand self-consciousness on the part of the reader. The risk is that every reading of Prynne becomes about the reading of Prynne – including this, inevitably.

So let us put things into perspective. Though I doubt Prynne's writing will ever achieve the renown of T. S. Eliot – it carries little of Eliot's appeal to an audience beyond the specialist – the reception of Prynne's work is reminiscent, on a smaller scale, of that of the *The Waste Land*, a poem variously praised or blamed while an industry sprang up to provide the footnotes. As I write these words in 2011, we are at a similar stage with Prynne. Though much reviled, Prynne's poetry is sending sympathetic scholars off on long expeditions in search of its origins, expeditions marked by a colonial fretting as to how much has been discovered versus how more there is to discover (i.e. how 'partial' they are). To be clear, I am not judging these efforts as futile. On the contrary, they are necessary. But unless we believe Prynne's intent with his poetry has been mainly to set a giant crossword puzzle for clever, earnest men – and nearly all his readers in print are male – they will only take us so far. If a poem by an erudite author such as Prynne doesn't add value to the sources that furnish so many of its ingredients, then all we are left with is a series of prose propositions doing an impersonation of poetry. Scholars who merely reveal those sources (happily, Wilkinson goes a little further) are performing a necessary but insufficient duty.

The question, therefore, is not what thesis a given poem by Prynne can be inferred to espouse, but what makes that poem poetry. If I want to know about the relationship of *homo faber* to *animal laborans*, I'll turn to Arendt. If I want to know about cardiopulmonary resuscitation, I'll check it out on the internet. But if I want to have such knowledge transformed and transfigured so that it is no longer simply knowledge, or even knowledge dressed up in poetic phrases, I'll look to Prynne and others. And having done so, I don't want to see an artful re-presentation of the poet's learning, as if he were a postgrad who can't let go. If anything I'd like that learning to be suppressed in favour of the verse, to have the wiring hidden. I want the poetic result, the result as poetry. So my simple question for this chapter is, 'What's poetic about Prynne?' There is a more complex question about the morality and emotion in his poetry, but I'll come on to that later.

Needless to say, this claim to the 'simple' question on my part, a simplicity opposable to the 'complexity' of Prynne/Wilkinson, is the oldest trick in the book. Besides, there is a Brechtian ethos in modern(ist) poetry, a version of suspending disbelief, that asks all artworks to reveal their wiring (Brecht being another reference – number 34 on my list – that Wilkinson adduces, by quoting Prynne on 'BB' in relation to Adorno – who would be number 35).[3] Is there not something perfectly appropriate about the Wilkinson reading that brings so many references to the fore, on the grounds that they are so pervasive in Prynne's verse?

Yes and no. Prynne's commitment to an admittedly idiosyncratic version of Marxist materialism indicates that, on the one hand, poetry should wear its means of production on its sleeve. And not just by bringing its manifold references up close to the surface, but by stipulating that the poems themselves be published in limited editions by small-scale publishers, so that the reader, flipping through a stapled pamphlet, is made undeniably aware of where they have come from. We get a dogged assertion of matter. And yet the bones of that matter sit within the flesh of something else – something 'poetic' – that I'll endeavour to describe.

I said that I would add to the bones myself, by highlighting further references or allusions or sources, and this I'll do as one way of coming alongside the poetic qualities of Prynne's poem. The first is Yeats' 'Leda and the Swan':[4]

A sudden blow: the great wings beating still
Above the staggering girl, her thighs caressed
By the dark webs, her nape caught in his bill,
He holds her helpless breast upon his breast.

How can those terrified vague fingers push
The feathered glory from her loosening thighs?
And how can body, laid in that white rush,
But feel the strange heart beating where it lies?

A shudder in the loins engenders there
The broken wall, the burning roof and tower
And Agamemnon dead.

    Being so caught up,
So mastered by the brute blood of the air,
Did she put on his knowledge with his power
Before the indifferent beak could let her drop?

It's in the words they share that the connection between the Yeats
and the Prynne is most obvious: 'blow', 'loosen(ing)', 'how can',
'rush' and 'air'. Then there is the overwhelmingness of the attack
that begins with the blow, though the single-sentence structure and
the non-sequitur clauses of the Prynne give it the greater ballistic
impact. Thirdly, both poems are governed by rhetorical questions.
Fourthly, the clash of abstract with concrete, especially somatic,
vocabulary works in both as an organizing device. And perhaps
most importantly, we have in both poems a juxtaposition of the
violent with the aesthetic, Yeats through the link to Helen of Troy,
who was the offspring of this mythological rape (and over whom
Agamemnon went to war), Prynne through the 'lyrical and joyous'
effects to be performed even in the midst of an assault (one thinks
of the Dachaulied).

But the issue is not whether these poems in some wise treat of
violence and beauty – that's hard to dispute – but whether they
themselves are violent and/or beautiful, a possibility they both flirt
with; hence the link I mentioned between the poetic and the moral.
And on this the two poems diverge. 'Leda and the Swan' exhibits
a haunted fascination with the moment of touching of the human
by the divine, and wants to stand close by it, as if, by proxy or

osmosis, some of that experience might rub off on the poet, Yeats. As if, moreover, the poet's place is defined as a blessed propinquity, like that of an angel or of Oedipus approaching the Sphinx. For all the gravity of its theme, all the hefty classical stonework with which it has been constructed, it is a naive or superstitious poem that goes beyond relaying the matter of mythology, albeit in re-wrought form, to levering itself into that mythological space in the hope that, like a tuning-fork, it will pick up the vibrations. It has a magical belief that the poem, by writing about mythology, can take on certain mythological properties. Sure, the poem wants to have moral force, even to inspire awe, but that magical belief militates against it, dispersing any moral force it might have gathered. This happens mainly because the question it poses at the climax – 'Did she put on his knowledge with his power/ Before the indifferent beak could let her drop?' – is too theoretical, and because theoretical, theatrical. The question lacks grounding in moral reality, and so comes over as poetical speculation, wanting in urgency. And so we have a tame poem about violence that aspires to be somewhat more violent than it is, in the belief that such violence would enhance its beauty or aesthetic impact.

The Prynne poem, by contrast, rolls up its sleeves and gets in among the action, inhabiting (which is not the same as condoning) the violence it depicts with conviction and even some relish. Any speculation has been vacuum-sealed out of it – the rhetorical questions, for example, ('how can this/ be done so strongly without/ the highest fidelity', 'had you not better with a metal spike') seem to be practical, if grainy in their resolution. Having said that, the poem asks for answers, and there is an enquiry that runs through it, concerning, for example, the relationship between sense and sound. The point being that this poem thrusts an active moral 'spike' into the world, less because it prompts the reader to worry about the terror that lies within beauty and vice versa, than because it makes a deep cicatrix in time. What do I mean by this?

To begin with, there is the sheer innovation of the poem (and other poems in Prynne's oeuvre) relative to the poetry it succeeds. If 'A blow on the side of the mouth' 'refers' to previous poets and other cultural artefacts, it also incorporates and surpasses them with such velocity, ambition and integrity that it could be claimed the poem refers to nothing at all, or makes at most the ghost of a reference. The references become under such conditions more like traces of the poem's speedy passage than phenomena to pause at. There is a profound disjunction, like a crevasse, with what has gone before, made by a 'blow' to the history of the lyrical and the joyous (and made apparent in the abrupt shift from the double dactyls of the first line, so promisingly classic, to the rebuffing spondees of 'strike harder'). This makes the poem intervention rather than supervention, cutting *across* poetic tradition, not prolonging it, its 'axis of attention' lateral, not vertical. Or to be more subtle about it, 'A blow on the side of the mouth' preserves the tradition of authentic poetry as the cutting across of itself.

In so doing, the poem exposes the openness of time, and with it time's readiness to host that which is surprising, new or different. Put the other way around, there is much less resistance in the forward movement of history to innovation than one might have thought, because time itself is permissive, and the poem exploits this weakness by way of a thoroughgoing modernity. The fact that the references, such as they are, appear to carry equal weight among each other, means that they collectively sink *away* from the surface of the poem, paradoxically giving that poem the feeling of having being written on a carte blanche. While on that surface the poem thematizes violence, there is a primary violence in its constitution, which is this invasion and occupation of the territory held open by history. And so the poem restarts history on a bias, with dogma, force, assertion, and a founding authority. It is easy to fall into the trap of taking Prynne's poetry to be heavily determined, defined and delimited by its sources, but what most determines it is itself – in this sense of taking advantage of history's openness to create something unprecedented and therefore apparently unnatural. It takes on a burden of risk and responsibility that the Yeats poem, distracted by a fantasy about a myth, avoids. It puts out a spike.

So if my guiding question is 'What's poetic about Prynne's poetry?', the first bit of the answer is that it is radically innovative – innovative to the point of noticing there was a tear to be made in the fabric of time, and then making it. Having done so, the poem and its poet find themselves in open country, unsheltered by the comforts of morals or mythology, forced to take responsibility for inventing and asserting substitutes for them, with all the violent arbitrariness that implies. What is poetic is this spike of moral singularity, and it makes the poetry, despite its critical air, surprisingly affirmative. The poem prevails in its novelty and difference, in the risk it takes to strike a blow upon the orders of poetry, to make poetry sing with a voice so original that it is exposed, but not cut off: it is still searching for a moral centre, with the poem's self-control keeping it a good distance from anarchy, anomie or alienation.

With these thoughts in mind, I'd like to add a second reference – or a 37th, depending where you count from – and develop the theme of violence and responsibility. Just as the 'parts/ of the soul' might refer to the division of the soul into three parts (reason, appetite and spirit), that Plato makes in *Republic*,[5] so 'A blow on the side of the mouth' appears to allude to the *De Anima*, to the eighth chapter in Book II, on hearing, where Aristotle stresses that sound is the result of a percussion, or a blow:[6]

> Actual sound is always of something in relation to something and in something: for it is generated by an impact. Hence it is impossible for one body only to generate a sound – there must be a body impinging and a body impinged upon; what sounds does so by striking against something else, and this is impossible without a movement from place to place.

Sound is the result of sensuous impact between two bodies, at least one of which has to move; it is a response to a kind of wounding, to paraphrase another of Prynne's titles – 'Wound Response'. In so far as it is a sonorous object, a poem clamours with such grievance. But again, just because 'A blow on the side of the mouth' *thematizes* the relationship between sound, poetry and hitting, does it mean the poem itself can be said to be the result of such an impact? And in any case, the poem on the page makes no actual sound, even if it is meant to be read aloud – it is as mute as a painting, 'for there is no cry'. I have just been arguing that Prynne's poetry has an autochthonous quality, a quality of having sprung up from nowhere despite such deep roots: so in relation to what other 'body' has the mute sound of this poem, this body, been made?

I think the word 'body' itself offers a clue. There is a basic point to be made, itself a version of materialism, that applies across much of Prynne's work, which says that all things lyrical and joyous, indeed all moments of affect, have a biochemical basis in the brain and the body housing it. On a broadly Nietzschean argument, all moral judgements can be traced to physical preferences, whereby 'good' equals 'I like this feeling' and 'bad' equals 'I don't'. That is how it would be possible to hold back the parts of the soul by black thuds: the soul could be traced to specific parts of the brain, spine or eyes and/or the neurochemical system connecting them. Such a reading would also provide some purchase on the phrase 'axis of attention' used in psychophysical studies analysing the operation of signals in the cortex; a reading that is not especially sophisticated or groundbreaking, even if the poem does little to discourage it. Just as basic is the cod version of Adorno – one of Wilkinson's many references – which says that fine art, including poetry, is not incompatible with extreme violence, and that, like a tragic flaw, the latter is even built into the Enlightenment project. On which grounds, one construes the poem as the transcript of an interrogation and torture, with the music of Mozart lilting and tripping in the background. But what about the idea of a profound identity between a poem and the speaking or singing body? Even as it is being smacked in the face, the body in the poem emits panicked gasps, these being the most primitive form of sound – not 'communication' but reaction to attack, the sucking in and blowing out of oxygen, and the urge to stay alive. As soon as one has breath, one has a resonance of the ribcage, a link with the mouth (which can be blown across from the side like the top of a bottle to produce sound), and then from the mouth to the ears, whereby the body becomes a sounding device, an instrument or poem growing more, not less, articulate under stress. To get sound out, there has got to be some pressure, and pressure cannot be found in the kingdom of the innocent.

In short, there is no world worth its salt that can come about without the force of arbitrary, artificial, even violent intervention: both the poem and the body, which at a certain point merge, sound out this force. Not that it's simply aggression – it is affirmation and productivity. Perhaps this explains the uncanny feeling of mercy that runs through the poem's account of an otherwise merciless battery, the letting-off before any killing and the switching to the relatively soothing 'as a form/ goes on through' – and with this we return to where the poeticism of the poetry might reside. What does this poem do that a plain narrative prose account of an attack, garnished with footnotes, could not do? Apart from formal elements – the shape of the poem, the indentation of the lines, the oddly bungled prepositional constructions like 'hardly as to know/ is to loosen' and 'in nor time or at all' – we are as readers put into a curious affective space. It is a space in which our own cognitive distress, caused by the effort to understand the poem, has little choice but to act the mirror to the poem's own account of cognitive disruption, caused by the blows. And with the cognitive function effectively scrambled (and without any 'I' in the poem to anchor the words) something else can 'go on through'. Fear gets transformed into a bracing, joyous energy, as if adrenal liquids rose to a certain level and then dilated or changed colour. Elements of sadism and masochism aren't purified out – the poem is no straight-forward sublimation of terror into beauty – and yet it is not fear that, by excluding everything else, wins the day. The energy isn't all negative. Nor are we quite invited to collude or collaborate with the violence, hence that merciful distance. Prynne is opening up the narrowest of moral passageways through the body, through the body of the poem, in which true morality begins with a departure from innocence.

So the poem sings with its body, with the materiality it cannot transcend and should not disavow, even if it might wish to dissolve into a purer sound, a higher fidelity. And so it asks searching questions of us, the reader, about our own being implicated in 'violence', and the degree to which our innocence has been compromised. If it has, that is no cause for damnation, but rather the opportunity to start again on a new bias, in which evil becomes a catalysing agent for good.

NOTES

Notes to Introduction

1 Heaney, S. (2010), *Human Chain*. London: Faber and Faber, p. 19.

2 See Mellors, A. (2005), *Late Modernist Poetics: From Pound to Prynne*. Manchester and New York: Manchester University Press.

3 Prynne, J. H. (2009), *Streak-Willing-Entourage-Artesian*. London: Barque Press, p. 1.

4 Celan, P. (1995), trans. M. Hamburger, *Poems of Paul Celan* (new edition). London: Anvil Press Poetry, p. 241.

5 Mallarmé, S. (1945), *Oeuvres Complètes*. Paris: Gallimard, pp. 457–77.

6 Marjorie Perloff, 'Reading Gass Reading Rilke', http://epc.buffalo.edu/authors/perloff/articles/rilke.html.

7 Duffy, C. A. (1985), *Selected Poems*. London: Penguin in association with Anvil Press Poetry, p. 115.

8 De Man, P. (1984), *The Rhetoric of Romanticism*. New York: Columbia University Press, pp. 152–3.

9 Leavis, F. R. (2008), *The Common Pursuit*. London: Faber and Faber, pp. 48–9.

10 Mark 12.41–44.

11 Abraham, N. (1994), 'The Phantom of Hamlet *or* The Sixth Act, *preceded by* The Intermission of "Truth"', in N. Abraham and M. Torok, trans. N. Rand, *The Shell and the Kernel*, vol. 1. Chicago and London: The University of Chicago Press, pp. 187–205.

Notes to Chapter 1

1 Tomlinson, C. (1985), *Collected Poems*. Oxford and New York: Oxford University Press, pp. 136–7.

2 For further discussion of white, red, violence and beauty, see my chapter 'White over Red', in Rowland Smith, R. (2010), *Death-Drive: Freudian Hauntings in Literature and Art*. Edinburgh: Edinburgh University Press, pp. 82–107.

3 Auden, W. H. (1991), ed. E. Mendelson, *Collected Poems*. New York: Vintage International, p. 273.

4 As quoted in Marshall, D. G. (1989), review of D. T. O'Hara 'The Romance of Interpretation: Visionary Criticism from Pater to De Man', *Comparative Literature*, vol. 4, No. 2, 204.

5 See the chapter 'Ezra Pound and the Fate of Vegetable Money,' in Hyde, L. (2006), *The Gift: How the Creative Spirit Transforms the World*. Edinburgh: Canongate, pp. 219–75.

6 Pound, E. (1977), *Selected Poems*. London and Boston: Faber and Faber, p. 53.

7 Eliot, T. S. (1969), *The Complete Poems and Plays of T. S. Eliot*. London: Faber and Faber, p. 171.

8 I refer of course to the essay, 'Tradition and the Individual Talent', in Eliot, T. S. (1951), *Selected Essays*. London and Boston: Faber and Faber, pp. 13–22.

9 Creeley, R. (1991), *Selected Poems 1945–1990*. London: Marion Boyars, p. 117.

10 Blackmur, R. P. (1981), *Language as Gesture* (Morningside Edition). New York: Columbia University Press, p. 6.

11 Davie, D. (1992), *Purity of Diction in English Verse and Articulate Energy*. London: Penguin, p. 196.

12 Forrest-Thompson, V. (1978), *Poetic Artifice: A Theory of Twentieth-Century Poetry*. Manchester: Manchester University Press, p. 20.

13 Empson, W. (2004), *Seven Types of Ambiguity*. London: Pimlico, pp. 33–8.

14 Probably the most helpful resource for those unacquainted with Heidegger's work in this domain will be Heidegger, M. (1975), trans. A. Hofstadter, *Poetry, Language, Thought*. New York, etc.: Harper and Row.

15 Walcott, D. (2007), *Selected Poems*. London: Faber and Faber, p. 106.

16 Heidegger, M. (1975), trans. A. Hofstadter, *Poetry, Language, Thought*. New York, etc.: Harper and Row, p. 152.

Notes to Chapter 2

1   Lowell, R. (1974), ed. J. Raban, *Robert Lowell's Poems: A Selection*. London and Boston: Faber and Faber, p. 101.

2   See Freud's discussion of the subject in his paper, 'Project for a Scientific Psychology', in Freud, S. (1958), trans. J. Strachey et al., *The Standard Edition of the Complete Psychological Works of Sigmund Freud*, vol. 1. London: The Hogarth Press and the Institute of Psycho-Analysis, pp. 283–397, especially p. 356.

3   Eliot, T. S. (1969), *The Complete Poems and Plays of T. S. Eliot*. London: Faber and Faber, p. 13.

4   Tomlinson, C. (1985), *Collected Poems*. Oxford and New York: Oxford University Press, p. 217.

5   MacNeice, L. (1979). London and Boston: Faber and Faber, p. 499.

Notes to Chapter 3

1   Hughes, T. (2003), *Collected Poems*. London: Faber and Faber, p. 1065.

2   Plath, S. (1981), ed. T. Hughes, *Collected Poems*. London and Boston: Faber and Faber, p. 212.

3   See Freud's discussion of the subject in his paper, 'The Theme of the Three Caskets', in Freud, S. (1958), trans. J. Strachey et al., *The Standard Edition of the Complete Psychological Works of Sigmund Freud*, vol. 12. London: The Hogarth Press and the Institute of Psycho-Analysis, pp. 289–302.

4   Plath, S. (1981), ed. T. Hughes, *Collected Poems*. London and Boston: Faber and Faber, p. 245.

5   Freud, S. (1958), trans. J. Strachey et al., *The Standard Edition of the Complete Psychological Works of Sigmund Freud*, vol. 12. London: The Hogarth Press and the Institute of Psycho-Analysis, p. 296.

6   Derrida, J. (1987), 'Cartouches', in trans. G. Bennington and I. McLeod, *The Truth in Painting*. Chicago and London: The University of Chicago Press, pp. 183–253.

7 Keats, J. (1970), ed. M. Allott, *The Complete Poems*. New York: Longman, p. 533.

8 Stevens, W. (1987), *The Collected Poems*. New York: Alfred A. Knopf, pp. 193–4.

9 Plath, S. (1981), ed. T. Hughes, *Collected Poems*. London and Boston: Faber and Faber, pp. 158–60.

Notes to Chapter 4

1 Ashbery, J. (2008), *Collected Poems 1956–1987*. New York: The Library of America, pp. 474–87.

2 Ibid., pp. 690–1.

3 See Bloom, H. (1997), *The Anxiety of Influence: A Theory of Poetry* (2nd edition). New York and London: Oxford University Press.

4 Yeats, W. B. (1982). *Collected Poems*. London and Basingstoke: Macmillan, p. 168.

5 Hill, G. (2006), *Selected Poems*. London: Penguin, p. 103.

6 For an invaluable analysis of the subject, see Clark, T. (1997), *The Theory of Inspiration: Composition as a Crisis of Subjectivity in Romantic and post-Romantic Writing*. Manchester and New York: Manchester University Press.

7 Yeats, W. B. (1981), *A Vision*. London and Basingstoke: Macmillan.

8 Bonnefoy, Y. (1991), trans. J. Naughton, *In the Shadow's Light*. Chicago and London: The University of Chicago Press, pp. 52–3.

Notes to Chapter 5

1 De Man, P. (1979), *Allegories of Reading: Figural Language in Rousseau, Nietzsche, Rilke and Proust*. New Haven and London: Yale University Press, p. 130.

2 Thomas, D. (1988), ed. W. Davies and R. Maud, *Collected Poems 1934–1953*. London: J. M. Dent and Sons, pp. 18–19.

3 Bunting, B. (1978), *Collected Poems* (revised edition). Oxford and New York: Oxford University Press, p. 71.

4 Mallarmé, S. (1945), *Oeuvres Complètes*. Paris: Gallimard, pp. 457–77.

5   Ibid., pp. 54–5.

6   Ibid., p. 27.

7   This is Henry Weinfield's translation in Mallarmé, S. (1994), *Collected Poems*. Berkeley, Los Angeles and London: University of California Press, p. 45.

8   Lawrence, D. H. (1977), eds. De Sola Pinto, V. and Warren Roberts, F., *The Complete Poems*. Harmondsworth: Penguin, p. 697.

Notes to Chapter 6

1   For this and the following references to uses of the word 'darkling', I am indebted to the resource – and especially its search function – provided online by the Poetry Foundation: www.poetryfoundation. org.

2   Keats, J. (1970), ed. M. Allott, *The Complete Poems*. New York: Longman, pp. 528–9.

3   Tennyson, A. (1989), ed. C. Ricks, *Tennyson: A Selected Edition*. Harlow: Longman, pp. 445–6.

4   Arnold, M. (1978), ed. M. Allott, *Selected Poems and Prose*. London, Melbourne and Toronto: Dent, pp. 88–9.

5   Hardy, T. (1978), ed. D. Wright, *Selected Poems*. Harmondsworth: Penguin, pp. 218–19.

Notes to Chapter 7

1   Tennyson, A. (1989), ed. C. Ricks, *Tennyson: A Selected Edition*. Harlow: Longman, pp. 351–2.

2   I am referring to Eliot's comments on Blake: 'We have the same respect for Blake's philosophy [...] that we have for an ingenious piece of home-made furniture', in Eliot, T. S. (1951), *Selected Essays*. London and Boston: Faber and Faber, p. 321.

3   Milton, J. (1971), ed. J. Carey, *Complete Shorter Poems*. London and New York: Longman, p. 239.

4   Larkin, P. (1988), ed. A. Thwaite, *Collected Poems*. London and Boston: The Marvell Press and Faber and Faber, pp. 208–9.

Notes to Chapter 8

1 Hopkins, G. M. (1986), ed. C. Phillips, *Gerard Manley Hopkins*. Oxford and New York: Oxford University Press, p. 128.

2 Ibid., p. 129.

3 Ibid., p. 181.

4 Ibid., p. 168.

5 Ibid., p. 142

6 Ibid., p. 110.

7 Ibid., p. 133.

8 Ibid., p. 150.

9 Ibid., p. 167.

10 Ibid., p. 135.

11 Ibid., pp. 132–3.

12 Heraclitus (1981), ed. C. H. Kahn, *The Art and Thought of Heraclitus: An Edition of the Fragments with Translation and Commentary*. Cambridge, etc.: Cambridge University Press, p. 85.

13 See Kant, I. (1987), trans. W. S. Pluhar, *Critique of Judgment*. Indianapolis: Hackett.

14 Hopkins, G. M. (1986), ed. C. Phillips, *Gerard Manley Hopkins*. Oxford and New York: Oxford University Press, p. 166.

15 Ibid., p. 166.

Notes to Chapter 9

1 Symons, A. (1989), ed. R. Holdsworth, *Selected Writings* (new edition). Manchester: Carcanet, p. 31.

2 Eliot, T. S. (1969), *The Complete Poems and Plays of T. S. Eliot*. London: Faber and Faber, pp. 175–6.

3 Baudelaire, C. (1975), ed. C. Pichois, *Oeuvres Complètes*. Paris: Gallimard, pp. 23–4.

4 Symons, A. (1919), *The Symbolist Movement in Literature* (revised and enlarged edition). New York: E. P. Dutton and Company.

5 Donne, J. (1933), ed. H. Grierson, *Poetical Works*. London, New York, Toronto: Oxford University Press, p. 15.

6   Eliot, T. S. (1969), *The Complete Poems and Plays of T. S. Eliot*. London: Faber and Faber, p. 14.

7   Symons, A. (1989), ed. R. Holdsworth, *Selected Writings* (new edition). Manchester: Carcanet, p. 32.

Notes to Chapter 10

1   Larkin, P. (1988), ed. A. Thwaite, *Collected Poems*. London and Boston: The Marvell Press and Faber and Faber, p. 165.

2   Ibid., p. 180.

3   Ibid., p. 184.

Notes to Chapter 11

1   Prynne, J. H. (1999), *Poems*. Newcastle upon Tyne: Bloodaxe, p. 377.

2   Wilkinson, J. (2010), 'Heigh Ho: A Partial Gloss of *Word Order*'. *Glossator* ('Practice and Theory of the Commentary: On the Poems of J. H. Prynne'), 17, 295–325.

3   Ibid., 320.

4   Yeats, W. B. (1982), *Collected Poems*. London and Basingstoke: Macmillan, p. 241.

5   Plato (1961), ed. E. Hamilton and H. Cairns, *The Collected Dialogues, including the Letters*. Princeton: Princeton University Press, pp. 683–8.

6   Aristotle (1984), ed. J. Barnes, *The Complete Works of Aristotle* (revised Oxford translation), vol. 1. Princeton and Oxford: Princeton University Press, p. 667.

INDEX